The Official
Sexy Solitary Suicide

★★★★★ Highly recommended!

"How do you write a book about depression that isn't too depressing? Author Winchinchala tackles this subject and elucidates how depressed people are often shunned by those closest to them and how difficult it is for those who reach out to them to understand and discuss this taboo. It's depressing!

Winchinchala opens the closet to this subject by discussing events from her own life and the lives of some notable icons who also suffered from depression, some of whom committed suicide. The gem, for me, in this book, is how Winchinchala introduces the reader, from a 1st person perspective, to the inner world of emotional pain that accompanies depression and the darkness and utter dread that engulfs the suffering psyche during those times.

One also becomes acquainted with a different, often overlooked aspect of depression experienced by many sufferers, that of frustration. Many depressives are endowed with a creative aesthetic perspective on life, which they express through art, such as writing, music, poetry, painting, or politics. Winchinchala refers to them as 'beats' (i.e. nonconformists, as opposed to 'sheep' - conformists), and she identifies as a beat. Beats are not necessarily depressed, but they often find themselves identifying socially with a counter-culture.

Her 'out of the box' angle on life is most eloquently depicted in masterful prose as she leads the reader through the high's and low's of some of the good times and numerous bad times she has had. Her beat persona is also reflected in the book's title, *Sexy Solitary Suicide* along with the cover illustration, which would make a sheep wonder, Why the juxtaposition of this quirky title and strange cover illustration with the depressing topic of depression? Her 'beat-ness' is further illustrated in poetic reflections in a number of poems at the back of the book.

The Official SEXY SOLITARY SUICIDE, written by a person who has lived through depression and recovered, will certainly resonate for those who stand at that precipice, and it will, hopefully, motivate them to stay in life and work through their aching psyches. In addition, this book provides valuable insight for all the psychotherapists who endeavor to understand the hell-hole their patients are in when they are clinically depressed."

Dr. Rick Lindal,
Psychologist in private practice,
Ontario, Canada;
www.dr-ricklindal.com
Author of:
"Slice of Life: A Self-Help Odyssey: A Practical Perspective for
Thriving Within the Trappings of the Physical World."

★★★★★ Highly recommended!

"In The Official SEXY SOLITARY SUICIDE, Winchinchala voices something that needs to be understood about depression. Her particular perspective is brilliant. I plan to recommend it to clients and students."

Allison Lee Axinn, Therapist
Regression and Dream Therapy,
Pietrasanta, Italy

newtoninstitute.org/life-between-lives-therapist/allison-lee-axinn/11/

★★★★★ "Very helpful."

That is what I, Winchinchala, hear from "survivors."

Winchinchala

Winchinchala is the first-born daughter of Seawolfe, Sagamore of a tribe of the Wôpanâak (Wampanoag) Indian Nation and Joy of European ancestry. Studies, work and curiosity have taken her to numerous distant ports. Their cultures, histories and myths inspire her work. Many of her fictional characters are affected by familial dysfunction an area with which, she confesses she is "sadly too familiar."

At Columbia University in the City of New York she earned a B.A. in Cultural Anthropology and an MFA in Film/Writing. There, she won the Warner Brothers' Award for *The Tea Party*, a screenplay. Later her play, *Remote Man* was runner up for the prestigious New England Clauder Playwriting Competition. For almost a decade she was a beloved professor at Berklee College of Music in Boston. Her favorite classes to teach were Film Grammar and Screenwriting. The previous decade she taught at Boston University.

The Official SEXY SOLITARY SUICIDE is a departure from her usual
Historical Fiction,
THE LIFE & LOVES OF MARINER JACKIE VIK (1940's)
A LITTLE CITY INDIAN IN THE 1950'S
or ONLY HUMAN SHORT STORIES

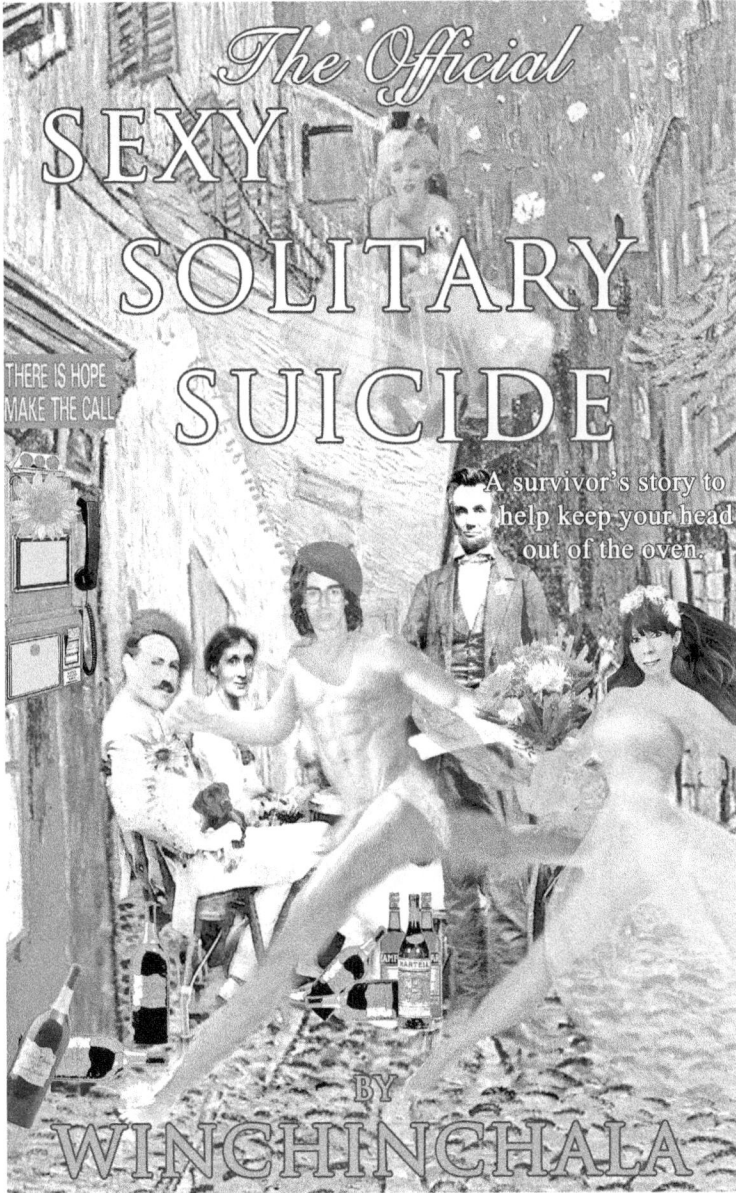

Also by Winchinchala

FICTION

ONLY HUMAN SHORT STORIES
THE LIFE & LOVES OF MARINER JACKIE VIK
A LITTLE CITY INDIAN IN THE 1950'S

SELECT TV /SCREENPLAYS

NEENEEMOOSHA SWEETHEART
SEINFELD Episode: "Schleppen Feathers" (1997)
REMOTE MAN, a play ©1990/publication 2002
SAVING GRACE (1982)
THE TEA PARTY (1979) Winner of Warner Bros. Award

SELECT VIDEOS

writer/producer/director: Winchinchala

THE EMPRESS DOWAGER'S ROBE (2001)
REFLECTIONS OF AN EVENING (1999)
YOUNG LOVERS' CHRISTMAS COWBOY CAVIAR (1998)

The Official

SEXY
SOLITARY
SUICIDE

*a Survivor's Story
to Help Keep your Head
out of the Oven*

Kindly purchase new, not used, editions for they alone benefit the author.

Caution: Professionals and Amateurs are herby warned: *The Official SEXY SOLITARY SUICIDE* being fully protected under the copyright laws of the United States of American, the British Commonwealth, including the Dominion of Canada, and all other countries of the Copyright Union, is subject to royalty. All rights and television broadcasting, and the rights of translation into foreign languages, are strictly reserved. Particular emphasis is laid on the question of readings, permission for which must be secured from the author, Winchinchala wsv6 [at] columbia.edu

This book is a combination of fiction and non-fiction. Properly recounting historical events requires the inclusion of historical figures and actual events. In instances of the author's autobiographical stories, actual persons, were renamed and altered to protect their identities.

Printed in the United States of America.
Library of Congress Cataloging-in-Publication Data
Library of Congress Control Number: 2010915733

Winchinchala

The Official Sexy Solitary Suicide, ISBN 978-1-889768-30-4

Book Design/Cover, original art by *Winchinchala*

Official Edition: 2017

DEDICATED TO:
Those who suffer from depression

Contents

REFERENCE

🌸 Artwork & Photo List

Acknowledgements

Tabatne Keihtánit
(Thank you to the Great Spirit)

Previously working drafts of this book were inadvertently released into the publishing stream. If you bought one, let us know and we will gladly exchange it for the "Official Sexy Solitary Suicide."

Paul Simon Music in New York for permission to include the lyrics to his brilliant classic; *I am a Rock,* © 1965. (p. 169)

The *Loukas Family of Massachusetts*: Kimon was a gentle spirit and a gifted poet. I consider it an honor to include his poem, "On Fields of Force: Boston Commons 4: A.M."

Thank you to the Samuel L. Bickford Family of Bickford's Inc., for taking time to find the historic photographs of the Hayes Bickfords cafeterias in Boston. One, nicknamed, "Coffee Corner" or "The Bic," was a major meeting place in the Beat scene.

 Dr. S.L.N., of Brookline MA., a kind, thoughtful, worldly, sensitive being, whose wisdom, patience, generosity and humor help me to understand the bizarre workings of the human mind, and to see myself in a brighter light, so I can continue writing and living.

David Howland, (1959-2015) of Pennsylvania & Yokahama, Japan for his intellectual insights, musical genius, mirthful conversations and incredible lightheartedness. (RIP)

Yiannis (John) Courduvelis of Lexington & Nemea, Greece for his poetry and lyrics, and who, on numerous occasions, saved my texts from evil computer viruses and operator ignorance. He also served as the male model for the cover,

Dr. Wayne Dyer, (1940-2015) philosopher, motivational speaker and prolific self-help author. While accredited with many words of wisdom, a couple of quotes really resonate with me.

"Be miserable. Or motivate yourself."

"How people treat you is their karma; how you respond is yours."

The year before he passed, he called me out of the blue. He expressed appreciation for my recounting of my experience with the angel Garbriel. I had been on the fence as to whether or not to include it. He encouraged me to do so, and I did.

I owe an incredible debt of gratitude to therapists, Allison Lee Axinn of Italy and Dr. Rick Lindal of Canada for their careful psychological reading and their feedback.

And friends, you know who you are, who accept me for who I am, "sadness, madness and all."

❋ Notes to the Reader

Book Cover:

Books on depression usually feature bleak, grey landscapes filled with rain and craggy silhouetted trees or people bent and weeping. I wanted something different. In Vincent van Gogh's "Café terrace in Arles, at Night," Ernest Hemingway holds a black dog, Virginia Woolf sits beside him. Abraham Lincoln stands tall in the background while beautiful Marilyn Monroe perches on the roof with her dog Maf. I am in the foreground running with a friend.

Book Focus:

Depression falls into many categories: Major Depressive Disorder (MDD)[1]; Bipolar I and Bipolar II; psychotic depression; seasonal affective disorder (SAD); Dysthimia, a milder long-term form of MDD and depression that accompanies Post Traumatic Stress Disorder (PTSD). The Official Sexy Solitary Suicide focuses only on MDD and its attendant PTSD.

Book Organization

At the end of several chapters are blurbs entitled "Notes" or "Analysis" or "Thoughts." Theses are Winchinchala's personal reflections or observations.

Repetition:

Yes, it is frowned on in fiction, but Winchinchala deliberately utilizes repetition, to reinforce or drive home certain points.

---

[1] MDD or clinical depression causes a persistent feeling of sadness-usually two weeks or more--and can lead to a variety of emotional and physical problems. A sufferer has trouble doing normal day-to-day activities, and sometimes feels life isn't worth living. (Mayo Clinic)

Political Correctness:

Today, it seems, thespians, male and female alike, prefer the term "actor." Actress is out. Politically correct terms have evolved for many words; for example, First Person, African American and woman are in, and American Indian, Negro and girl are out etc. However the latter are used to accurately reflect their respective time periods.

Images:

Winchinchala has always preferred books with images. She has personally selected or created those included herein.

Inner Monologue:

There are different approaches to representing inner monologue, meaning dialogue when a character speaks to herself. People With Wings prefers *italics*, not quotes.

Our readers are smart; they will get it.

Quality:

In order for books to print-on-demand, they have to fit in the standard cookie cutter format. Thus with the flick of a button, an inkjet printer can generate a particular book anywhere on the planet. As a result, publishers are at the mercy of the distribution company's equipment, and they report, "The print quality of the final product varies widely."

www.facebook.com/peoplwithwings [sic]

* Notice:

While researched and quoted, the perspectives on mental health stated by the author, Winchinchala, are for informational purposes only and not intended as specific psychiatric/medical advice or a substitute for professional psychiatric medical treatment or diagnoses.

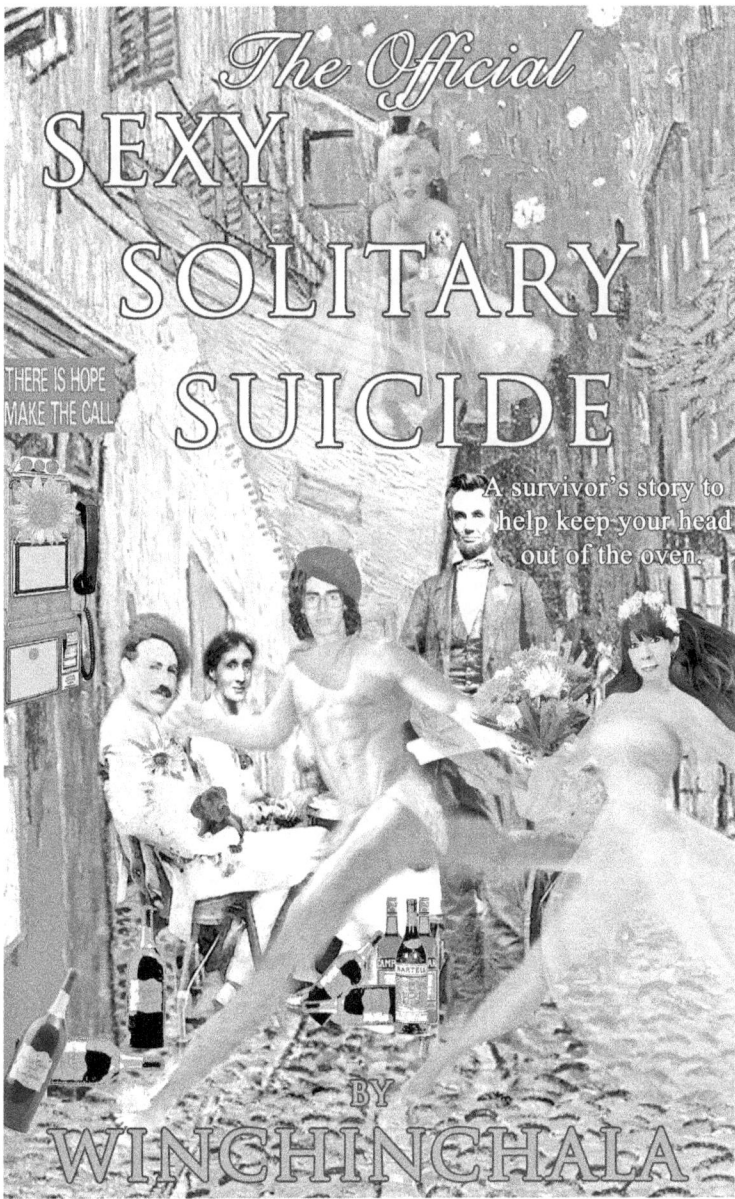

The Official
SEXY
SOLITARY
SUICIDE

THERE IS HOPE
MAKE THE CALL

A survivor's story to
help keep your head
out of the oven.

BY
WINCHINCHALA

So You're Looney Tunes

Oh No. Killed yourself?
The Ultimate Guide to life After Death

Depressed? Snap out of it already

Wine & Whiskey, the Drinking Man's Cure for the Blues

Choose to be Happy, the Way of Denial

The Science of Depression

The Biology of Sadness & Happiness

Bulletproof Couchfree psychoanalysis

You're not crazy, just nukkin' futz.

Dear Reader,

To start, I confess, I am neither a scientist nor a psychologist; I am, perhaps like you, a person who suffers from the demon depression,[2] and one who knows others suffocated by its crushing weight. Over the last many decades, depression has been part of my life. Often have I bent the ears of friends and strangers on the subject; most were very interested and suggested I "write about it." (Maybe they were just trying to get rid of me.) The problem was, writing on the topic didn't appeal to me. I am a story teller, one plagued by characters who I enjoy bringing to life. I felt writing on the demon would be too painful; I didn't want to be involved, but dammit, I am. To date, I have lost nine people to suicide; my mother and grandmother among them. In the lingo of psychiatry, that makes me a "survivor." I am also an "attempter," for the demon has lured me into its inky, fetid abyss to meet my own end. I wanted to bury all that, pretend it didn't exist, not dig it up and concretize it in black and white. However, in the end, I decided what I had learned and experienced might help another person. I wrote the facts and truths in the way I know best, as a story teller.

After all, 18%[3] of the adult population of the United States suffers from depression, many more if children and teens are included. Unfortunately ignorance of the disorder, fear and the powerful stigma surrounding it often stand in the way of sufferers seeking help. Everyday, 94 people in the U.S., some as young as five, relieve themselves of what has become the agony of living. Wandering depression's pitch black valleys for weeks or months, searching and hoping for a way out is utterly painful and exasper-

---

[2] I refer here to Clinical Depression or Major Depressive Disorder MDD. It is different from the blues or the grief of losing a loved one or being down as a side effect of a medical condition. According to psychiatric references, MDD is a *persistent* state of despair, (longer than a couple of weeks) accompanied by a sense of worthlessness, extreme fatigue, insomnia or hypersomnia, anhedonia and/or recurring thoughts of suicide.
[3] The National Institute of Mental Health.

ating. My goals are: to empower sufferers, so they will seek help and inform the 82% who are allegedly not depressed, so they might not shun them, be more tolerant, learn to speak to them. A mixture of the best intentions and ignorance causes those who don't know about the seriousness of depression to dole out their cures of cups of tea and positive thinking to beat the blues to the clinically depressed or they assail them with unhelpful platitudes about tomorrow being another day, perhaps the last thing depressives wants to hear because unless they get help, that dawning day promises to be as dark and painful as the past 102. What then does one say? Providing answers to that question is another of my goals. Taboos are destigmatized by giving them a voice. Society now widely accepts the word "vagina" and discussions of Beyonce, Jennifer Lopez and Kim Kardashian's asses but not depression. We can change that, be more accepting.

Research for this book and the therapy in which I have been engaged revealed certain truths. First, I too am depressed. I honestly never knew. I had always been sad, always. I thought everyone was sad. Second, to treat depression, one must find its source/s in order to cope, not to be happy. Happiness was never guaranteed, understanding that allowed me to accept myself for who I am, to find peace in my heart. Third as I studied depression's history, causes, treatments and sufferers, and I discovered, it is one of those riddles, wrapped in a mystery, inside a golf ball or something. It is a merciless, sadistic immortal hellion that delights in torturing humans' psyches, thrives on their anxieties, savagely quaffs their tears and sucks the marrow from their souls, but it can be managed and even beaten. It can. Once I accepted that, I became as proactive as I could, and I survived.

If you find something in this book sheds a ray of light on the darkness, helps you understand yourself or a sufferer motivates you to persevere, then I would be glad.

Wishing you Strength and Peace
Winchinchala
Santa Fe, New Mexico
2017

PART I

Depression
Overview - Treatment – Cases- Causes

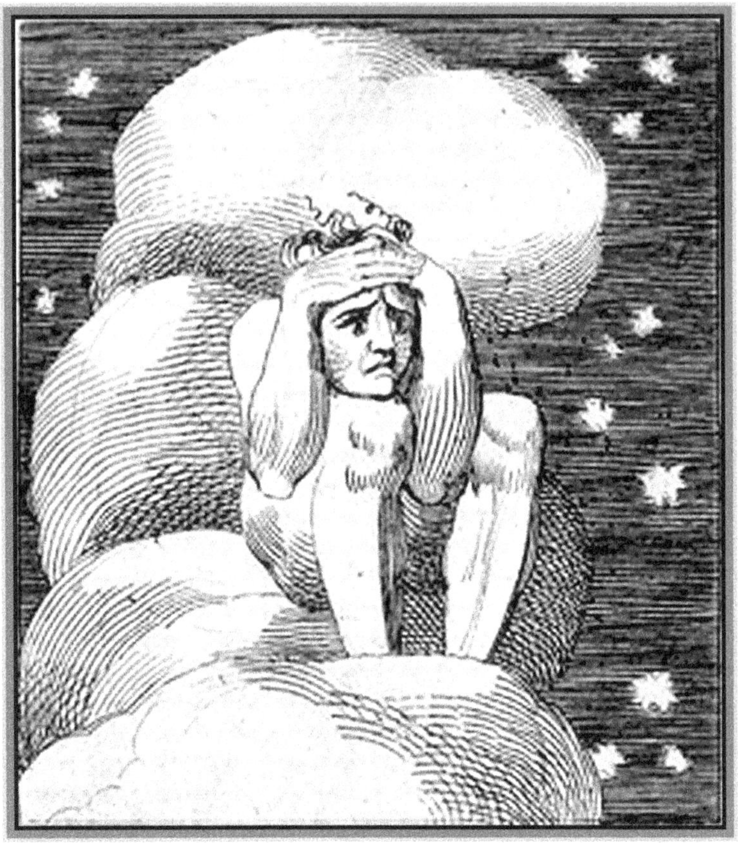

🌼 1. A Survivor's Infinite Quest
my Mother

By the time I was a freshman at Columbia University, suicide had taken my maternal grandmother and two close friends, and then, during my first semester, it took my young mother. Her self-inflicted death devastated me. It also launched me on a quest for answers. Why do people take their own lives? Why had my mother taken hers? I grew up in a children-should-be-seen-not-heard environment. Adults told children what they thought they needed to know, and that was very little. As a result, my mother's physical and mental health were a mystery to me. I only knew what I saw, a beautiful woman who, I later learned, was the quintessentially perfect 1950's wife. With her fair hair coiffed and her lips creamed with bright red lipsticks, she ran the house and minced about prettily dressed in her favorite colors, pastel blue or green. Depending on the shade, her hazel eyes would change to match them, but they always sparkled. One September night, three weeks after classes had begun, I was dining out with my fiancé and a few friends. The feeling I had forgotten something gnawed at my nerves. *Was the stove off? The iron unplugged? What?* As I was usually right about such feelings, I excused myself and rushed back to our apartment nearby to see what was amiss. Nothing. Still, something held me there. Suddenly, my mother appeared in a psychic flash. *Should I call her?* The phone rang. I answered and heard her voice. Intuitively, I knew she was taking her life. I wanted to hang up and call the police. *What are they going to do? She is thousands of miles away.* So I wrapped my hand tightly around the receiver as if it was her hand and holding it would save her. My soul writhed. I could not speak. I pressed the receiver tightly against my ear to better hear her every word. I was scarcely breathing. She slurred, "Are you there little girl?" I emitted a barely audible "Mmm hmm," and she continued with fading love-laced messages for me to pass along to my father and brothers. I wanted to take notes, but my pen was on my desk in the other room; the phone cord would not stretch that far, and I simply could not let go of the receiver. As it turned out, writing was unnecessary. Her soft, sweet voice was burning her words into my brain. When she stopped, I imagined the sparkle flickering and dimming in her eyes. I heard her lips pressing around her cigarette filter and ice clinking in her glass. She exhaled. I heard the glass thud on the carpet. The emotion of the moment weakened the bones in my legs, and I dropped onto the ottoman in a heap. I concluded she had fallen asleep. I wanted to say *Mother*? The word was stuck on the tip of my tongue in a saliva of fear. Several painfully long moments passed. I was still unable to hang up. I placed the receiver on the ottoman and left. I returned to my fiancé and friends, but I had lost my appetite.

I ghosted through the next day on autopilot. After classes, my fiancé greeted me with an uncharacteristically, troubled face. "Bad news. Your mother died yesterday." I stood there benumbed. He held out his arms, but I walked to the other room comfortable in the knowledge that, My *mother is asleep. How could she be dead? I just talked to her.* My lack of reaction about anything over the next days encouraged him to repeatedly ask, "Are you all right?" I thought I was, but I no longer enjoyed anything. Usually, we reveled in the vibrant New York entertainment scene, but at stellar performances of "A Chorus Line," "Clams on the Half Shell" and "Chicago, an American Musical," I sat in the chair like a shawl. Apathy dulled planning our wedding; I stopped. Friends, who noticed, chalked the change up to grief.

Her death took with it many feelings that to this day have not fully returned. I did not cry over her death, at least not then. How could I when I did not accept it having happened? Why had she taken her life? Why hadn't she gotten help? Why had she called me? Why hadn't I saved her? Decades-long research and eventual therapy taught me the following: Attempters often reach out for help or because they do not want to die alone. Those who are truly determined to end their lives can not be saved; they usually make sure of that. Their reasons will never make sense to survivors or even other attempters.

Dr. Carl Jung summed depression up as an "abaissement du niveau mental," a lowering of the level of consciousness, a mental and emotional condition experienced as "loss of soul." I agree, for when I fall into a depression, I not only feel empty, but also that time has slowed down,[4] making the sadness seem interminable. The horror, guilt, helplessness and abandonment that arose from having shared my mother's last moments heightened my anxiety born of earlier traumas and threw me deeper into the depths of darkness. Her death had disinterred one of my bonafide secrets; the kind a person tells no one, not even herself. I too had tried to

---

[4] Sven Thönes, Daniel Oberfeld, "Time Perception in Depression: a Meta-Analysis," Journal of Affective Disorders, 04/ 01/ 2015, V.175, Pages 359–372

commit suicide, more than once. Listening to the lullaby of her voice, I ached to be with her, to hold her, for I knew exactly how she felt. Even now, all these years later, I am sometimes filled with a loss of soul that urges me to join her.

"The pathological sequelae[5] following a suicide are tremendous;"[6] and according to many psycho-therapists, it is an event from which most children never full recover, especially if the victim is a parent. The bond is so great, it can also cause a child's desire to be with the parent to override the survival instinct. For example in 1945, August DeMont and his five-year-old daughter, Marilyn jumped from the Golden Gate Bridge[7] in San Francisco. She went first and willingly, according to witnesses.[8] Had she simply wanted to be with him or obey him or did she want to die? Contrary to popular belief, children, as young as five, can feel the depths of hopelessness required to commit suicide, and they do understand the meaning of death.[9] In 1954, Charles Gallagher and his son of the same name leaped to their deaths. Charles senior was first, and a few days later Charles junior followed. His note read, "I am sorry. . . . I want to keep dad company." Why hadn't the adults gotten help? At that time, successful therapy was scarce, and the stigma against those having such thoughts was very powerful.

Though the stigma is slightly weaker today; it remains and is a deterrent to those seeking help. It forces them into silence and hiding where they try, often to no avail, to deal with the depression themselves. Even professionally treated, MDD can hang on for years. As Virginia Woolf wrote in *Orlando*, "all extremes of feeling are allied with madness." True. If one eats, sleeps, talks, drinks, travels, fornicates or whatever to excess, one is viewed as

---

[5] Pl. of sequela, a condition that stems from another.

[6] Harvard University's Douglas Jacobs, a suicide expert in clinical practice.

[7] A location associated with suicide it opened on May, 1937. Since Harold Wobber leaped to his death, more than 1700 have followed.

[8] Children ages 5-9 are not immune to suicide. On average about 33 children a year take their own lives according to the Centers for Disease Control and Prevention.

[9] Arielle H. Sheftall, et al. "Suicide in Elementary School-Aged Children and Early Adolescence," Journal of Pediatrics, 9/2016.

not "normal." Society allows for a certain amount of eccentricity in creative circles but not among "average" people. Until the 1970's, those who behaved in a manner perceived as abnormal by a neighbor, family member or anyone, could be reported and removed to an asylum... indefinitely.

At times doctors, under the auspices of the CIA, would use some institutionalized patients as guinea pigs, inject them with viruses or drugs or subject them to experimental doses of electroconvulsive therapy, ECT. In addition, because institutions had bare bones staffs, they were left to their own devices and were known to abuse the weak and vulnerable. Involuntary commitment was so wide-spread in the 1950's that "559,000 people in the United States were in-patients[10] in mental facilities. They were

held but not cured. The fear of being picked up and locked away was grounded in reality. As with others, my mother expressed concerns about institutionalization. They escalated in 1961 after actress Marilyn Monroe's harrowing experience. Her New York psychiatrist, Dr. Kris had advised she get rest and misled her into believing she was going to a spa-like facility, not a mental hospital. There, Marilyn was stripped naked and whisked off to a padded cell. The "inhumane" treatment she later reported, contributed to the culture of fear that existed among those with

---

[10] Grob, Gerald, N., The Mad Among Us: A History of the Care of America's Mentally Ill. New York: Free Press; 1994.

mental struggles. In letters to her California psychiatrist, Dr. Greenson Marilyn wrote,

"...I felt I was in some kind of prison for a crime I hadn't committed. The inhumanity there I found archaic ... everything was under lock and key...the doors have windows so patients can be visible all the time..."

In the institution, doctors dismissed her complaints, and insisted she was "sick, very sick." The call she was finally allowed to make was to her devoted ex-husband, baseball-player, Joe Di-Maggio. As if in a scene from *One Flew Over the Cuckoo's Nest*,[11] the uber controlling head nurse refused his request to sign her out. Joe's well-known response was to holler, "I'll give you five minutes to get her out here, or I'll tear this f–king place apart brick by brick." Post-haste, Marilyn, was delivered to him. Immediately, he escorted her to the better-funded Columbia-Presbyterian Medical Center where she received more appropriate treatment. "If that could happen to a star..." my mother mused. Marilyn's life has been excavated and dissected in 600 plus biographies since her death. The orphaned girl turned actress turned sex kitten icon still fascinates, especially when viewed through a psychological lens. Throughout her relatively short life, she was stalked by a justifiable fear of falling victim to mental illness. Her maternal grandparents lived out their lives in mental institutions, where her mother too had been placed on various occasions. Genetic inheritance of mental illness was a real possibility[12] for Marilyn, one compounded by her childhood environment. With her mother hospitalized, she was sent to foster homes where she claims to have been sexually abused.[13] The insecurity of being bounced around and the trauma of sexual abuse laid the foundation for her troubled psyche. Dr. Greenson diagnosed her with "borderline, addictive personality disorder." He felt that past, in part, had led to her extremes in behavior from depression to im-

---

[11] Novel by Ken Kesey highlighting terrible conditions of mental hospitals.
[12] Chances of inheriting mental illness on page 100.
[13] Effects of sexual abuse, see page 129.

pulsivity and recklessness. Indeed, her indiscreet sexual affairs could be considered quite dangerous. Among her paramours were Sam Giancana, a Sicilian-American mobster and his known enemies, President John F. Kennedy and his brother, Robert F. Kennedy, the U.S. Attorney General,[14] who were both married. However, for Marilyn, living on the edge was as much a part of her as being risqué. They went hand in hand with the public image of a star living the glamorous highlife. Thus, when she died, August 5, 1962, the public easily accepted the original coroner's assessment of "probable suicide." The police were "not so sure" and the foreign press declared her death a "murder."[15] The lack of clarity has inspired several conspiracy theories that continue.

My mother's passing inspired stories concocted by family to make her death less socially damning. One is that she had decided to take her own life after learning she had inoperable cancer. A second claims she was destined to take her own life because her mother had. She offered no explanation the night she called. She did ask me not to tell anyone in her family what she had done. She used her final breaths for messages to my father and older brother and to express concern about what would become of her soul. More than once, she had told me, "For Catholics, a person who commits suicide is destined to burn in Hell forever and all eternity." A man I knew reminded me of that after he had heard how she died. He smirked, swirled his drink in his glass and announced, "Well that's one less person in Heaven." His glib remark sent me to the bible to see how it handles suicide. By my count, half a dozen therein had taken their own lives,[16] and

---

[14] The actual extent of her involvement with President or Robert Kennedy is unknown. Probability for an affair with the latter was found in a letter from the men's sister, Jean Kennedy Smith.

[15] This is not solely my opinion. Mountains of evidence discredit the idea of suicide. In the Reference, are two supporting documents, one from the FBI.

[16] Samson (Judges 16:30); Saul and his armor-bearer (Samuel 31:4/5); Ahithophel (Samuel 17:23); Zimri (Kings 16:18) and Judas (Matt. 27:5). I have debated as to whether or not Abimelech (Judges 9:54) committed suicide because after a woman crushed his skull. He had his squire stab him to save him the humiliation of having been killed by a woman. (To me that is murder or euthanasia at best.)

in so doing had broken the sixth commandment, "thou shalt not kill." Judas hanged himself, and then he burst open in the middle and "all his intestines gushed out." It is assumed he went to Hell. King Saul also took his own life. Broken commandment, so straight to Hell, right? Not necessarily. Mitigating circumstances may have saved Saul, for he knew if the Philistines caught him, they would torture him to death. In a preemptive strike, he avoided that by killing himself. Based on the texts, God must have redeemed him because he ended up in Heaven with Jonathan. "In their death, they were not divided: they were swifter than eagles, they were stronger than lions."[17] My mother was a beautiful, innocent being with an innate, spiritual connection to the innocents of the world, animals and children. In my mind, that made her easy prey for the ancient soul-sucking demon, depression, and like Saul, she feared imminent pain. She had fought with the weapons available at that time, prayer and alcohol. The latter must have deepened her depression which eventually overpowered her, wrapped around her so completely that even her smallest breath was excruciating. She decided she couldn't take living. A few have declared her "selfish" for that. Nothing could be further from the truth. She was in pain. She knew her depression was affecting those she loved. She did not want to be a burden. That is what I choose to believe.

❀ The Journey Begins

One short week after my mother walked on from her existence, I was obsessed with answering the questions her death had raised. I asked my anthropology professor for permission to write a research paper on "suicide, though it might be more sociological." He assured me I was "safe. Bronislaw Malinowski[18] writes about suicide in the Trobriands." After the next class, he provided a surprisingly lengthy bibliography that ran across several disciplines. My eyes fell on the titles: *Le Suicide* by Émile Durkheim (1897),

---

[17] Samuel 1:23
[18] Bronislaw Malinowsi (1884-1942) British Cultural anthropologist.

The Savage God: A Study of Suicide (1971)[19] by Alfred Alvarez and *Suicide and the Soul* (1973), by James Hillman. Chills trickled down my spine and tears down my face as I left the room, but I was hopeful the books would explain the enigma of suicide. Stigma kept me folding and refolding the bibliography into a miniscule square that I tucked into my pocket, so no one would see it.

That afternoon at Butler Library, I gathered the first ten books, established, as mine, one of the plush soft-leather chairs in an infrequently traveled nook and dipped into the harrowing sea of knowledge. I had taken the first steps on my infinite quest that has, thus far, lasted over forty years. In that time, I have learned one thing for certain; the mind is a complete mystery. Certain readings reawakened my concerns for my mother's soul. For example, philosopher David Hume declared suicide "an affront to God." I decided the story of Saul had been missing from his bible and continued. Émile Durkheim, a sociologist, made me smile, for he got my mother off the hook! Her individual psychology had not driven her to a grim end, society had. The bums! "It takes a village" as they say.

Durkheim delineates four types of suicide in very broad categories: "Altruistic, Fatalistic Egoistic, and Anomic."[20] Altruistic is carried out when one is voluntarily overly socially integrated and holds the value of the society above oneself, for example a soldier who throws himself on a bomb to save the other troops. Fatalistic stems from one being restrained, forcibly integrated into society like a slave or a prisoner for whom death is the only way to be free. Egoistic emerges in those who have become detached from the society, their friends and family who would give meaning to their lives. Singles and seniors who outlive all their friends and serious drug addicts or alcoholics are among them. Lastly is Anomic suicide resulting from a lack of regulation/control due to life having been turned upside down by a disaster. *Mother could*

---

[19] Alfred Alvarez' cultural and literary examination of suicide that begins with a memoir of his friend, author Sylvia Plath.

[20] Emile Durkheim, *Suicide: A Study in Sociology* translated by John A. Spaulding and George Simpson, edited with an introduction by George Simpson, The Free Press, 1951, p. 14 & 15

have been in the Egoistic category, I thought. *Or perhaps she had too much money.* Durkheim also noted that, "Wealth...by the power it bestows, deceives us into believing that we depend on ourselves only," while "poverty protects against suicide because it is a restraint in itself."[21] (I am in awe of that concept.) Since the realization of human desires depends on the resources at hand, "the poor are restrained and hence less prone to suffer from anomie by virtue of the fact that they possess but limited resources."[22] Those who identify too highly with money and material goods fall into the Anomic category.

Notes:

Definition of Depression: As defined by the American Psychiatric Association, it is as a serious medical illness that can strike at any time. No mention of *insanity.* A charming expression for depression that Winston Churchill picked up from his nannies is that it is a "black dog."[23] When he became noticeably gloomy, he confessed, "I have a black dog on my back," to warn people to steer clear. Though Churchill had a flesh and blood dog, there was no confusion because that dog was not black.

Denial: "Not just a river in Egypt," as they say. Denial comes about when the unconscious mind wants to protect a person from a harsh reality. For example: A Casualty Notification Officer arrives at the home of a soldier. Upon seeing the officer's car, the wife or mother know that is a sign of bad news. Their heads automatically turn from side to side in denial of the truth they know is coming. Though the officer makes it clear that the soldier is dead, loved ones may refuse to believe it then and possibly forever. Denial is a powerful force.

Repression: Another unconscious defense mechanism by which the brain absorbs the upsetting reality and refuses to allow it to

---

[21] Ibid.
[22] Ibid
[23] Greg Arnold, *Churchill's Black Dog*, (1993).

process them. As I understand it, some conscious participation is necessary in repression. One must make an effort to keep those thoughts inside, and they can give rise to acute anxiety.

Fear of confronting the pain that a truth may cause can keep defense mechanisms in place for years, lifetimes even, but the cost is one's peace of mind and one's personality. It takes a lot of brainpower to sustain them. Imagine holding a shield up all day every day while you are trying to live your life. If one is willing to engage in therapy, one can be more proactive and consciously analyze the problem or cope with it.

"The Queen of Hearts she made some tarts
        All on a summer day:
The Knave of Hearts he stole those tarts,
        And took them quite away!"

"Now for the evidence," said the King, "and then the sentence."

"No!" said the Queen, "first the sentence, and then the evidence!"

"Nonsense!" cried Alice, so loudly that everybody jumped, "the idea of having the sentence first!"

"Hold your tongue!" said the Queen.

"I won't!" said Alice, "you're nothing but a pack of cards! Who cares for you?"

At this the whole pack rose up into the air, and came flying down upon her: she gave a little scream of fright, and tried to beat them off, and found herself lying on the bank, with her head in the lap of her sister, who was gently brushing away some leaves that had fluttered down from the trees on to her face.

"Off With Her Head!"

2. Treating the Mind
Ice Picks & Electrodes

Intangible memories that contribute to making the human experience delightfully heavenly and/or dreadfully infernal have a tangible home. They reside in the limbic system. The good, stored in our left frontal lobes, are made of the moments that fill us with warm pleasant feelings, bring smiles to our faces: new puppies, starlit kisses, sunny picnics on the beach, babies' first steps, family dinners and on and on. A scent, a phrase or an image can trigger one complete with its warm fuzziness, maybe even a glimpse in the mind's eye. The bad, stored in the right frontal lobe, are made of hurt, grief, rejection, embarrassment, shock, abuse, physical injury. Those we would rather forget, so our brains often bury them beyond easy access deep within its sulci (grooves). There, they morph into miniscule sea urchin-like creatures with hundreds of sharp, spiny, spikes that needle our nerves and heighten our anxieties.[24] If we could get our hands on those— Ha!—We could douse them in lighter fluid and send them into oblivion on the backyard hibachi. Damn urchins. What to do?

Ice Picks

Doctors in the 1940's and 50's tried to get rid of the nettlesome, metaphorical demons that manifested as major depression and other mental issues with electroconvulsive therapy (ECT) AKA shock therapy or with the lobotomy, ice pick therapy. The latter, extremely controversial from its inception, was a barbaric crapshoot that involved inserting instruments identical to ice

---

[24] A neologism coined by suicidologist Dr. Edwin Shneidman for unbearable psychological pain—hurt, anguish, soreness, and aching.

picks through a patient's eye into the prefrontal lobes. Egas Moniz, the Portuguese neurologist and inventor, who devised it, received a Nobel Prize in 1949 despite the fact that by then, several countries had already outlawed the gruesome procedure. Several patients died. Literally only a few improved of the thousands on whom the procedure was performed. All the rest ended up with seriously diminished mental capacities or as zombies.[25] Two high profile cases among those with catastrophic outcomes were those of the sisters of President John F. Kennedy and playwright, Tennessee Williams.

Rose Marie, "Rosemary" Kennedy was John F. Kennedy's sister who had been labeled as "mentally retarded" because she was les active and "slow" in school; however, her personal diaries from the 1930's,[26] demonstrate at least average language skills. Had she taken English in college, she probably would have passed. After all, the upper cutoff for mental disability was 69. Dr. Bertram Brown, a former director of the National Institute of Mental Health, wrote, "...that Rosemary could do arithmetic meant that her IQ was well above 75,[27]" and still other doctors have placed it closer to 90 which, depending on the test, is on the low side of average, *not* "mentally retarded." Kennedy family biographers agree that Rosemary Kennedy was notably "the most beautiful" of the clan's girls. While the observation smacks of sexism today, it was then appropriate, for a lovely appearance was a great asset to a young society woman intent on marrying well. Had she had any apparent mental defect, Joseph P. Kennedy, patriarch of the prominent, political Kennedy family, would not have promoted her participation in Britain's highest social circles when he served as United States ambassador to the Court of St. James in England. He did so proudly, without any limitations, and she was well sought after. In fact, she was among the debutantes, carefully selected, to be "presented" to King George VI and Queen Elizabeth

---

[25] A corpse said to be revived by witchcraft.
[26] *Rose Kennedy and Her Family- The Best and Worst of Their Lives and Times*, Gibson, Barbara & Ted Schwarz. Birch Lane Press, 1995.
[27] Ronald Kessler, *The Sins of the Father: Joseph P. Kennedy and the Dynasty He Founded*. Grand Central Publishing. 1996.

in 1938 for whom she executed a flawless curtsey. The following year, with her entire family, including her father, young Rosemary attended the investiture of Pope Pius XII.

Kathleen, John F. & Rosemary Kennedy

At the outbreak of WWII, the Kennedy sons reported, as expected, for military duty. The daughters were sent to college, except Rosemary; she was sent to a convent in Washington D.C. After having sipped freely from the heady brew of London society life, convent life was incredibly bland. In the spirit of students bored and boarded everywhere, she allegedly spiced up her evenings by slipping out, unescorted. Such behavior for a young woman, particularly one from a "good family," in the 1940's was viewed as disgraceful. Though Joseph Kennedy had affairs with actress Gloria Swanson and his personal assistant and held pro-Nazi views, it was his daughter's nighttime antics he feared would threaten the lofty political goals he had set for his boys. Without telling anyone, not even her mother, he arranged for the lively Rosemary to be among the first in the country to receive a lobotomy to quell her urges. It did. In fact, "it reduced Rosemary to a babbling two-year-old invalid who would henceforth be incapable of intellectual advancing.[28] Joseph P. Kennedy callously hid the procedure and his formerly gorgeous, giddy daughter from his family and the world behind the excuse that she had decided to join the convent. As far as he was concerned, the operation was a success. In a letter to the institution where the surgery was performed, he expressed his gratitude. "I am still very grateful for your help. . . . after all, the solution of Rosemary's problem has been a major factor in the ability of all the Kennedy's to go about their life's work and to try to do it as well as they can."[29] (Hmpf.)

A second such catastrophic act was carried out on Tennessee, (Tenn) Williams' older sister Rose. Along with Daikin, whom he calls "my improbable little brother," they grew up in a household made dark and tense by their abusive, alcoholic father and depressed mother. Daikin, perhaps due to being nine years Tennessee's junior, escaped "blue devils" as Tenn called his own neuroses, including deep depression. With copious amounts of alcohol and amphetamines, Tenn managed and carried on to become one of America's greatest playwrights, wining a Tony, a Pulitzer Prize and numerous New York Drama Critics Circle Awards. His sister, Rose, with whom he had a deep relationship was his "muse." She was featured in several of his works, most notably, "The Glass Menagerie," but she too had blue devils. They manifested in a plethora of symptoms possibly misdiagnosed as schizophrenia. Anthropologist Roy Richard Grinker notes that in the 30's, "children were being lobotomized," especially those who were described as living in fantasy worlds—then called schizophrenics, but who would today almost certainly be called autistic."[30] Did her bouts of hysteria and profanity amount to either? Had she actually abused herself with altar candles or was she telling her mother that to get a rise out of her? A rise she got. Deeply embarrassed and at a loss for what to do with her daughter, Mrs. Williams took Rose "to the head doctor, and demanded

---

[28.] Ibid.

[29] Amanda Smith, ed., Hostage to Fortune: The Letters of Joseph P. Kennedy, N. Y, Viking, 2001, Goodwin, The Fitzgerald's and the Kennedy's, 745.

[30] Clay, Morton, "Not Like All the Other Horses: Neurodiversity and the Case of Rose Williams," The Tennessee Williams Annual Review, p. 107

they, 'Do anything,' she repeated 'any-thing to shut her up!'"[31] Anything was a lobotomy that Tennessee's described as having "tragically becalmed Rose," his "vibrant muse."[32] Rose's level of functioning remained high, yet she too spent the rest of her days in an asylum. Both women were in their early 20's, so they didn't even have fully developed brains[33] when they were subjected to the extreme treatment for little more than mischievous behavior and a mental disorder, perhaps autism. Tragically, the price they paid was their brains, their lives.

❀ Electrodes

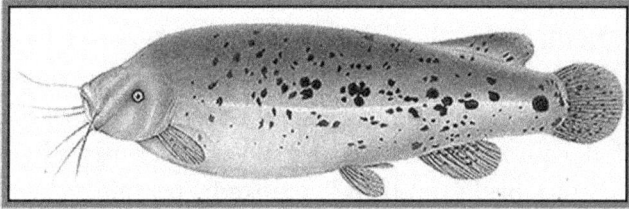

In 1938, another method for controlling mental problems came on the scene, shock therapy. The idea of influencing brain activity with electricity emerged around 4000 BC in ancient Egypt. There, fishermen observed when a Nile catfish was in their nets, they could not touch other fish without getting hurt. Unbeknownst to the Egyptians, the Nile catfish has an electrogenic organ that can generate electric shocks of more than 450 Volts.[34] Eventually, they

---

[31] Interview with Dotson Rader. "The Art of Theater No. 5." *Paris Review* 81: 145–85. Rpt. in Conversations with Tennessee Williams. Ed. Albert J. Devlin. Jackson: UP of Mississippi, 1986. 325–60

[32] Tennessee Williams, *Memoirs*, 1975, p. 126

[33] (Research studies in neuroscience find that the human brain grows for, at least, twenty-five years.) Giedd, J. N., J. Blumenthal, et al. (1999). "Brain development during childhood and adolescence: A longitudinal MRI study." Nature Neuroscience 2 (10): 861-863.

[34] Jaakko Malmivuo and Robert Plonsey, Bioelectromagnetism Principles and Applications of Bioelectric and Biomagnetic Field, New York, Oxford University Press, 1995

harnessed that power and used it to anesthetize pain. This was later documented in the 17th century by visiting Jesuit missionaries. Another application of electricity to the brain shows up in 1804 when "Luigi Galvani, a professor of Physics at the University of Bologna, performed electrical stimulations on the exposed human cerebral cortex of recently decapitated prisoners which evoked horrible facial grimaces."[35] This proved that the cortical surface could be electrically incited and gave rise to further research into its application for the therapeutic treatment of neuropsychiatric disorders. How the electric current was working was not clear, not even by the 1940's when doctors were using it on people with severe mental illnesses. All they knew for certain was that between 75 and 470 volts, similar to that of the Nile fish, zapped into the brain induced a grand mal seizure.

It is worth noting that the current normally operating within a human brain is a miniscule fraction of that. The impact of such an intense jolt caused patients to thrash so violently, their hearts stopped, limbs broke and jaws cracked. To minimize physical harm, doctors modified the method and dosages, but patients reported loss of intelligence and amnesia. While Dr. Harold Sackeim, PhD, the main proponent of the procedure, dismissed their complaints, neurosurgeons John Friedberg and Sidney Samant confirmed that ECT absolutely causes memory loss and damages brains in the same manner as head injuries. Dr. Frank Vertosick likened ECT to "attempting to repair a computer with a chainsaw.[36]" Sackeim, held his ground until 2007 when he finally concurred that ECT causes permanent amnesia and permanent deficits in cognitive abilities that affect individuals' ability to function."[37] To be fair, over time, the procedure was refined, and a few patients sing ECT's praises. Carrie Fisher, an actor and Kitty Dukakis, wife of former Massachusetts governor and Presidential candidate, Mike Dukakis have accredited ECT with helping them.

---

[35] Ibid

[36] http://wellbeingfoundation.com/

[37] The Journal of Neuropsychopharmacology reported the results of the largest follow-up study ever done on ECT patients. January 2007

Notes:

For over forty years, there has been a Patient's Bill of Rights. It was generated with the expectation of ensuring patients are given considerate and respectful care and understandable information regarding diagnosis and treatment. Depressives who often suffer from anxiety need to try to be proactive and exercise their right to ask questions and take time—as much as they need—to consider the pros and cons of the recommendation/s put forth.

There are pills to be larger, pills to be smaller
And those that do nothing at all.

✿3. Pills:

Development, Use & Abuse

How to manage or diminish depression, no matter what the cause, has long eluded doctors. Were it not for serendipity, in the 19th century, they might still be looking for chemical treatments for bipolar disorder, BD and Major Depressive Disorder, MDD. In London doctor Alfred Garrod, an internist testing the effects of lithium on patients with gout, an inflammation of the joints, noted a marked elevation in their spirits. In France, doctor Roger Reyss-Brion observed there were but few "manic-depressives in Marseilles" where citizens freely drank a fizzy drink called Dr. Gustin's Lithium Salts[38]; it contained slightly higher lithium contents than the mineral springs whose waters had long been considered curative and prescribed by doctors around the world. Finally, in the 1950's, doctors from the U.S. to Denmark and Australia, conducted trials on the effect of lithium in treating mania. Results were mixed, many were uplifted, but there were several deaths—they realized—due to lithium's tendency to accumulate in the body. After adjusting the dose, the effects were more uniformly beneficial and doctor dispensed lithium liberally.

Patty Duke raved about lithium in her book, "A Brilliant Madness: Living with Manic Depression Illness." "It saved my life and it gave me life." Ms. Duke, an enormously accomplished actor of the Bobby Soxer[39] set, won an Oscar for her portrayal of Helen Keller in "The Miracle Worker" (1962) at just 16 before starring in "The Patty Duke Show." (1963) At that time, the stigma against mental illness was so strong that had the public learned of her problem, her career would have been ruined. Therefore, for dec-

---

[38] Reyss Brion, discussion, in Jean-M. Sutter, ed., "Psychopharmacologie," L'Encéphale 62, suppl. (1973): 68.

[39] Bobby Soxer: sociological coinage to describe music fans of the late 40's and 50's who attended sock hops.

ades, she secretly battled a ferocious, undiagnosed, mania that sent her into crazed rages during which she would hit her children; lavish foul-mouthed abuse on the world; shop without restraint; throw herself from moving automobiles; marry a stranger and attempt suicide, multiple times. Finally, in 1982, her need for help superseded her career and fortunately placed her in front of the right therapist. By then, the FDA had approved lithium, which her doctor prescribed. Far from killing her creativity, a side effect feared by many artists, it becalmed her. She continued to excel in acting and became a mental health advocate, all because doctors had observed the positive side effects of a drug for gout on patients' moods.

As with lithium, early pharmaceutical treatment for MDD came about by chance. From the 20's to the 40's, Amphetamine, aka Benzedrine, Dexedrine or Methedrine was a drug on a journey to find a disease, and as such, it was tested on a plethora of ailments ranging from dysmenorrhea to low blood pressure to respiratory distress and narcolepsy. The drug's intended effects of incited cognitive enhancement; increased energy and mild insomnia worked beautifully to stave off sleep which was essential for WWII soldiers and pilots who would have died had they succumbed to fatigue in the field. There were other positive effects as well, weight loss and elevated mood. Psychiatrists agreed with Dr. Abraham Myerson assessment that "...what we call sadness is to a large extent the disappearance of the energy feeling."[40] When "Time Magazine"[41] reported his findings that amphetamines, considered harmless "pep-pills," were effective not only in reenergizing depressives helping "regular people" recover from hangovers and low moods," its use skyrocketed. Within a few years, the United States buzzed in the throes of a full-blown, albeit legally prescribed, epidemic. While amphetamines did not cure anything, they certainly made people feel better; everyone was happily hopped up: truck drivers, students, athletes, housewives, jazz musicians, entertainers and even—it is rumored—

---

[40] Abraham Myerson, *When Life Loses Its Zest* (Boston: Little, Brown, 1925).
[41] Anon., "Trial and Error," *Time*, 14 September 1936, 33.

ahem, politicians. The FDA estimates that by 1962, more than 200 million amphetamine tablets were in circulation in the U.S.

"...*if the individual is depressed*..."

".... if the individual is depressed or anhedonic ... you can change his attitude ... by physical means just as surely as you can change his digestion by distressing thought ... *In other words, drugs and physical therapeutics are just as much psychic agents as good advice and analysis* and must be used together with these latter agents of cure."

Myerson, A.— *Anhedonia*— Am. J. Psychiat., July, 1922.

Only in the last decade has there been available—in Benzedrine Sulfate—a therapeutic weapon capable of alleviating depression, overcoming "chronic fatigue" and breaking the vicious circle of anhedonia.

Doctors prescribed them less and less for "depression" for ethical reasons and because newer, better antidepressants had become available, again by chance. Patients being treated for tuberculosis with Isoniazid reported an unexpected euphoria. That led to further research and the synthesis of Tricyclic Antidepressants (TCA's). These were better than stimulants because they effected changes in brain chemistry and communication in its nerve cell circuitry known to regulate mood. The downside was they affected other chemical messengers that triggered unwanted side effects such as weight gain, dry mouth, constipation, drowsiness, dizziness and cardiac conduction abnormalities that disinclined patients to continue on them. The positives were enough for neuroscientists to continue focusing on altering the brain itself.

Eventually, in the name of helping and for profit, they developed a host of Selective Serotonin Uptake Inhibitors (SSRI's), the most well-known are Zoloft, Paxil Luvox, Celexa and Prozac. They too had negative side effects such as sexual dysfunction, low sodium levels and suicide ideation but with such rarity that they were considered safe for all ages, Prozac in particular. In fact, it is so safe that it is one of the few drugs approved by the FDA for airline pilots.[42] Pharmaceutical companies welcomed SSRI's as a profitable product with a broad consumer base, and insurance companies welcomed them with the hope they would be a money-saving replacement for costlier talk therapy; they are not. Initially primary-care physicians had dispensing privileges, but their "limited training in diagnosing and treating mental health disorders[43] led the way for them to miss or misdiagnose complex psychiatric disorders."[44] The truth is, only a small percentage of depression is caused by the abnormal functioning of nerve cell circuits or biochemical imbalances that may be managed with medication. The rest are genetic or reactive, due to inter/transgenerational, physical or psychological trauma. Scientists' empirical data reveals these, in fact, capable of permanently modifying NR3C1, a gene that "affects a person's ability to deal with stress."[45] Psychotherapy ("talk therapy"), of which there are dozens of variations, helps identify the source/s of neuroses.

---

[42] Press Release – FAA Proposes New Policy on Antidepressants for Pilots". Faa.gov. April 2, 2010.
[43] General Medical Degrees, (MD) take 8 years. Psychiatrists 12. The additional 4 to focus on neurology and complete a psychiatric-specific residency to for certification from the American Board of Psychiatry and Neurology.
[44] Smith, Brendan, "Inappropriate Prescribing" Monitor on Psychology 6/2012
[45] News Editor, P. (2009). Child Abuse Alters Brain Gene. Psych Central.

As Dr. Marc Olfson[46] noted, greater effort needs to be placed on "increasing access to psychosocial interventions to treat symptoms and behaviors that are currently being addressed with antipsychotic medications." According to pharmaceutical sales, a whopping 11 percent of all children and teens are afflicted with Attention Deficit Hyperactive Disorder (ADHD) and are being treated with the most costly antipsychotic medications; Risperdal, Abilify, Zyprexa and Seroquel. Why? Meds alone neither identify nor address underlying issues if they are serious enough to require them. Perhaps the problem is simply their brains are not fully developed, and they won't be until 25 or so. Research indicates young people process information with the amygdala, the emotional part of the brain while adults process it with the prefrontal cortex, the rational section that responds with good judgment and an awareness of long-term consequences. "In teen's brains, the connections between the emotional part of the brain and the decision-making center are still developing—and not necessarily at the same rate, so when teens experience overwhelming emotional input, they can't explain later what they were thinking."[47] The "I don't know," they offer in response to "Why would you do something like that?" is genuine. In addition, children and teens are just that, children and teens, so they have the usual internal run-of-the-mill confusion and issues at home associated with growing up that cause them to act out. For example, J.D. Salinger's, Holden Caufield who declares, "I didn't exactly flunk out or anything, I just quit, sort of." Perhaps his apathy came about because he had lost his younger brother to leukemia and/or his hysterical mother was making him crazy. Or Tom Sawyer? "The harder Tom tried to fasten his mind on his book, the more his ideas wandered."[48] He couldn't focus because he was a daydreamer, or he wasn't engaged by the material, not because of ADD or ADHD. Today, the boys' teach-

---

[46] Olfson, Mark, MD, MPH, of Columbia University Medical Center (CUMC) and NYS Psychiatric Institute "Trends in Antipsychotic Medication Use in Children, Adolescents, and Young Adults," JAMA, 07/01/2015.

[47] *Health Encyclopedia*, Rochester Medical Center, 2017.

[48] Twain, Mark, *The Adventures of Tom Sawyer*, 1876.

ers may have referred them to counseling where, most likely, they would have been referred for medication. Nothing new really.

Drugs have always been used to control the feisty or disruptive in the society. Once upon a time, doctors readily prescribed the powerful barbiturate, Nembutal, as the ad read, "for the prompt sedation of rowdy kids." And while, once upon a time, heroin—yes you read that correctly—heroin, was medically pre

scribed to suppress coughs, parents used it for the non-medical purpose of supressing their children, so they themselves might have a bit of peace. What is alarming is the increasingly high number of children who are being medicated. An analytical study of recent data reveals that one in six[49] Americans over the age of six uses antidepressants or sedatives for mental health issues, when a little talking might be all they need. However, they along with pharmaceutical and insurance companies are more supportive of allegedly quick-"fix"pill solutions. As a result, the U.S. is, once again, in the midst of a legally prescribed epidemic.

---

[49] More, Thomas, J. and Mattison, Donald JAMA, 12/14/2016

Notes/Thoughts:

1. I am not in any way suggesting that all doctors, insurers and big pharmaceutical companies are all callous pushers of for-profit potions and pills? There are talented, compassionate, medical professionals committed to helping find what ails individual and to curing them. Penicillin and insulin stand out as two medicines that changed the course of health on earth. Indeed, the greed for profits shifted Health *Care* for *patients* to Health *Service* for *consumers*. Sufferer must be mindful, make and invest the time in themselves, be informed and selfish and take what they need from the system.

2. Having MDD, or any mental disorder, is not a choice any more than the biological color of ones eyes. However, sufferers can choose what to do about it. If one is suffering from MDD, one must ask oneself, "Do I want to find out how to treat this problem?" Depression and PTSD interfered with my daily life so much that I could not do anything. Medication was a start, but I needed to find a therapist.

Be proactive.

Ask questions.

If something doesn't work...

try something else.

It's your brain.

Get your money's worth.

The time has come, the Walrus said,
To talk of many things:
Of shoes and ships and sealing-wax
Of cabbages and kings
And why the sea is boiling hot
And whether pigs have wings.

"Through the Looking Glass," Lewis Carroll

4. The Power of Talking...
to the right person

"Silence about a thing just magnifies it."

~ Tennessee Williams

"When people refuse to speak out for too long, it's like water that's stagnant and starts to rot!"

~ August Strindberg

"Everything becomes a little different as soon as it is spoken out loud."

~ Hermann Hesse

Talk Therapy. Talk Therapy. Talk Therapy. What's the big deal? As Sigmund Freud writes, "Words call forth effects and are the universal means of influencing human beings.[50]" The power of the spoken word has proven truly magical in many cultures. Oral histories reveal that for at least a thousand years, the Scotch-Irish, French and Native Americans had "fire doctors" capable of talking fire out of a person's burn.. Talking to fire? Yes. Anthropologists report, "The belief is so strong, that when a person receives a burn, even a serious burn, the community sends for a fire doctor, and will let no one do anything at all to relieve the injured."[51] Furthermore, Catholics seek out ordained priests to hear their confessions and forgive their sins in the name of Jesus Christ. The psychological benefit of confession, according to Freud, is that the telling relieves a person's "oppression and does him good."[52] The religious, of all denominations, and the secular verbalize

---

[50] Sigmund Freud, a General Introduction to Psychoanalysis, Stanley Hall President, Clark University, Boni And Liveright Inc New York, 1920. p.3.
[51] The Frank C. Brown collection of North Carolina Folklore Volume six Durham, North Carolina Duke University Press 1961.
52 Sigmund Freud, The Question of Lay Analysis, Volume XX, 1926

prayers and wishes to saints, spirits and the universe. Requesters believe blessings or good fortune will come in response. That is true for depressives as well, but addressing the right entity is important. If simply talking worked, the depressed could talk to the universe, themselves, or their friends and families, as they, no doubt, do, but will they get a *right,* response? Persistent depression MDD, BP or PTSD are serious mental health issues, friends and family are unlikely to offer any cures. How could they? What do family and friends know? Can they, with certainty, tell an issue is the result of a head trauma or a physical illness such as hypothyroidism or hypoglycemia, too much iron, too many hormones or not enough or if its source is a deep childhood event that the depressive may not even remember? No. And if they venture to answer and it turns out they are wrong, then they have to suffer the consequences.

Except in cases concerning minors, all they can offer is well-meaning sympathy that neither lifts nor cures depression. The education and scripts we all receive growing up are for initiating and responding appropriately in life's predictable social circumstances, not diagnosing friends' mental health issues. Before expressing anger or frustration with a depressed friend or giving him advice, one must ask oneself, "What the heck do I know about treating depression?" Remember, grieving over the death of a person or animal, or just having the blues for a couple of days is not MDD. The safest thing to do is encourage focusing on diet and exercise, reading, going to group and seeking professional help? Don't encourage depressives to tell you what is wrong. Many don't know. And if they are sourced in taboos such as incest, childhood sexual assault, abuse by a family member, alcoholism or drug addiction, friends may be uncomfortable hearing about it and unable to process such disturbing information. A few may be struggling with issues themselves. In addition, listening to a loved one or friend trying to sort out mental health problems can take over one's life and even impart secondary trauma on them. In that way, mental illness can be contagious. One can express concern, but set boundaries, make lists of other topics. More on this is discussed in Part II, p. 133.

Therefore, both not knowing and knowing the cause are why many depressives are disinclined to socialize or talk. They clam up, and then do the worst thing they could possibly do, isolate. Behind a curtain of silence, they are prey to urchins (p.25) that poke their brain and release their unhealthy anxieties, thoughts of unworthiness, loneliness, hopelessness, especially hopelessness. What is a depressive to do? Find the right "fire doctor," so to speak, the professional psychiatrist or mental health professional with whom s/he can communicate. Why? It's just talk, right? Indeed. That is the function they fulfill. As Jacques Lacan, the renowned French psychoanalyst said, "Analysands are there to talk – to talk about anything."[53] Anything?! Yup. That's why, once upon a time, patients went to therapists five days a week, to freely associate, to perhaps arrive at painful childhood memories, the meaning of recent traumatic events, mistreatment, dreams etc. That approach is now considerably less popular. Very few have the inclination, the time or the finances to blather on endlessly. As with everything else, Talk Therapy (TT) now has a "let's-do-this" approach, and reams of empirical evidence indicate it works.[54].

I know this is not easy. Once one summons the motivation to get help—unless one has boots full of money—one has to navigate the mental health system to find that right person. It demands courage and determination. Depressives need to dig deep.

Thoughts:

> *"Be miserable. Or motivate yourself."*[55]

---

[53] Jacques Lacan, "The Triumph of Religion" p.63 from a press conference held in Rome on October 29, 1974, at the French Cultural Center.

[54] Jonathan Shedler February–March 2010, American Psychologist © 2010 American Psychological Association Vol. 65

[55] Dr. Wayne Dyer.

Swartz Piet

🌼5 *Suicide and Attempters' Tales*

"The thought of suicide is a great consolation:
by means of it gets one through many a dark night."
Friedrich Nietzsche

Humans have been taking their own lives since before recorded history. Why so much attention now? The increase in victims has reached "a thirty year high."[56] In 1999, U.S. Surgeon General, David Satcher focused his attention on this national tragedy and issued his "Surgeon General's Call to Action to Prevent Suicide."[57] The three pillars of his program are: Awareness, Implementation and Methodology (AIM) as well as recommended strategies "to reduce the stigma associated with mental illness;" and provide "comprehensive mental health coverage in insurance plans." Subsequently, the World Health Organization (WHO) launched an initiative on suicide prevention. The agency's three-fold objectives are: limiting depressives' access to the means of suicide, early identification of depression and follow-up by health care workers. While admirable, these goals are almost impossible to implement. The stigma, embarrassment and fear discourage depressives from coming forward. Even if they do, they are often not forthcoming, not even with professionals who along with the process are familiar. Some think the insurance companies will broadcast their secrets. Insurers do have need-to-know policies in place, but they are to authorize payment for treatments and medications for which only doctors' brief diagnoses are submitted not their in-depth notes.

Despite federal initiatives and non-profit prevention plans the suicide crisis rages on. In 1999, there were 29,199 suicides. The

---

[56] "U.S. Suicide Rate Surges to a 30-Year High," *New York Times* 4/ 22/ 2016.
57 Satcher, David, "Call to Action to Prevent Suicide, 1999."

last time an agency took count in 2014, there were 42,773.[58] A call to action to prevent suicide is needed now more than ever. The rise is attributed, in part, to rampant drug addiction, isolation, the Internet and social media[59] and life's stresses of which there are many. One is extreme economic difficulty as was seen on October 24, 1929 when the stock market crashed. Masses lost absolutely everything. The suicide rate hit an alarming 18.9 per 100,000 from the previous year's 12.1 per 100,000. One reporter wrote, a person "had to stand in line to get a window to jump out of."[60] However, suicide is not reserved for those who lose all their material goods. Indeed, suicide cut through the entire society during the Great Depression; the rate climbed to 22 per 100,000 or almost 27,000 deaths per year in the U.S. Yet, interestingly, when stable times returned, the suicide rate continued to rise.

Wait a minute. Humans are biologically hard-wired to survive, and many face stress every day without gruesome thoughts of killing themselves ever crossing their minds. What's up with that? Most likely their brains are filled with balanced chemicals and normally functioning neurons, the basic working unit of the brain and nervous system. In order for the brain and body to work, its neurons have to communicate with each other which they do via neurotransmitters, electrical impulses and chemical signals. The chemicals are, very basically explained—because I remind you, I am not a scientist—Dopamine, Glutamate and Serotonin. Respectively they control movement, help information stream to the front of the brain, boost chances of a neuron firing when necessary and enhance the electrical flow among all the brain's cells. When chemical messages are miscommunicated among neurons, depression can occur. If it is serious enough, thoughts of suicide seep in. Depressives and attempters are not "crazy" or even mentally ill. Their circuits are misfiring.

To endure an overwhelming sense of despair day in and day out for weeks or months brings on an excruciating psychache. Through the dark, murky lens of their exhausted imbalanced existences, depressives may see a future filled with that pain, one in

---

[58] Curtin, Sally C. M.A. et al. "Increase in Suicide in the U.S.," 1999–2014
[59] National Center for Biotechnical Information.
[60] Rogers, Will, in his column, October 24, 1929.

which they perceive themselves to be a tremendous weight on their families and friends. Unburdening those about whom they care of their own miserably depressed lives is the grim solution their psychotic[61] thinking proposes. There is nothing wrong with their survival instinct; in fact, it is repulsed by what ending their twisted thinking would bring. *What? Put a gun in my mouth, a noose around my neck, a razor in my vein, leap off a bridge or in front of a train or....* Psychosis and survival battle it out. The former insists, "Death is the best solution," but survival insists, "that is a bad idea, a very bad idea." Then one day, in a weak moment, impulse steps in and within five minutes[62] psychosis wins and makes their fatal decision. That is it. There are no exercises for our fragile, intangible brain cells or neurons; they can misfire in anyone. Depression does not discriminate.

A man I would have considered the least likely to even be capable of falling into a depression, let alone contemplate or attempt suicide, is Mike Wallace (RIP) of CBS's *60 Minutes*. His peers called him the "Pit bull reporter" and the "Grand Inquisitor" because of his "take no prisoners" style of "ambush reporting" and interrogation-like interview techniques. He could break through the defenses of the most challenging and most guarded of interviewees. In the course of his conversation[63] with the former Iranian leader the Ayatollah Khomeini, he told him his enemy, former Egyptian President Anwar Sadat, said he was "not a Muslim," but "a lunatic." Surprisingly, a genuine smile slipped across the Ayatollah's famous stone-face. Mike Wallace was bold and invincible, but then General Westmoreland sued him and CBS for libel. (Litigation, ranks among the top stressors.) Before his case went to court, CBS apologized to the General, and the suit was dropped. Nevertheless, having had his integrity publically assaulted hurled Mr. Wallace into a depression during which he attempted suicide.

---

[61] Psychosis is a brain-based condition that can result in nihilistic thinking bizarre perceptions (sight, sound), behaviors, and heightened emotions made worse by environmental factors, in particular drug abuse and stress.

[62] Research indicates it usually takes 5 minutes for an attempter to decide.

[63] CBS January 2008.

Luckily his wife found him before death had claimed his soul. He sought treatment. Then in keeping with "the old reporter's pledge to not only "afflict the comfortable[64]" but "comfort the afflicted," he shared his experience. At 1:30 in the morning on the Bob Costas Show," he told his story to the audience in which he thought a few "might have the same suicidal feelings" he had once had. Again talking proves helpful. The relief he felt after speaking spurred him on to talk more openly, for depression had dragged him down to a place he defined as "the bottom of the heap" where he saw no way out but suicide. It almost won, but it was overcome by the will to live. "I have to get out of here," he told himself. An assault on the integrity of an experienced reporter was almost his undoing.

I had a similar experience incited by a lawsuit. As stated, "litigation is one of the greatest stressors." Mine dragged on for years and years and triggered a major depression and long-dormant PTSD. My attorney advised me to try to get myself under control. I thought consulting a therapist at that time would make me appear mentally unstable, so I didn't. After all, I had just learned they could subpoena my psychiatric records. I tried to cope on my own. It was a daily chore in the face of colleagues' shunning me, their unexpectedly slanderous remarks and downright lies. It was disheartening to hear my hard won accomplishments, praise and awards denied by colleagues, many of whom I had considered friends. "Try not to take it personally," I was told. "They have to go along to get along, to save themselves." The spiny urchins tumbled in my brain, brought up gloomy days and interfered with my ability to function on a very base level. Every night for months, I fended off the desire to go to sleep... permanently. It was exactly as Nietzsche writes, "The thought of suicide is a great consolation: by means of it gets one through many a dark night." The following is one attempt, I pieced together.

---

64 Safer, Morley, "Remembering Mike Wallace 1918-2012" CBS News.com, April 26, 2012, 1:04 PM

***

Tuesday, February 18, 2003

Insomnia was torturing me. I had literally not slept for two nights. I watched the news which was all about the weather. A paralyzing Nor'easter had been slamming the east coast but was, at long last, allegedly heading out to sea. A record-breaking 27.5 inches had draped the city in a silencing winter white coat. Incredibly snow was again falling. Quite absent-mindedly, I took two sleeping pills with a sip of wine. Looking at the pile of pills on the table, I asked myself, *Didn't you already take those?* A draft called me into the other room to make sure the window was shut. I returned to the table and took two pills. My gag reflex caused me to pause. *Did I already take two? Or did I take four? If I did, now I have taken six washed down with wine. How many did I have to start?* I had no idea. Panic overcame me. I got up and paced frantically. *If I took six, is that enough to kill me? Was my subconscious telling me to kill myself?* I grabbed the phone and called a suicide help line. I was astonished when I got a recording. "This is the [Bla Bla] help line. No one is available to take your call at this time. If this is an emergency, please go to your nearest emergency room..."[65] I hung up. *A recording? Really?! Why would anyone think a person contemplating suicide would be able to get it together to go to a hospital emergency room? CRAP!*

A force welled up inside me and propelled me into the post blizzard no man's land. The snow was thigh-high outside the front door. I had to force my way through it to reach the sidewalk. The ploughs had been at work, so on foot the main streets were passable. Utterly alone, fueled by panic, I tromped madly for blocks. When the panic subsided, I was near the library in Copley Square, about a mile away. I stopped and watched the flurries flurrying. The damp, cold air bit through my heavy coat. I scanned the deserted streets for a place to warm up, but the state of emergency was still on. *Hotels never close. The Plaza is probably open.* As I headed down

---

65 Calls to the center inquiring why they use a recording when they advertise 24-7 help resulted in their admitting difficulty of round the clock staffing because they depend on volunteers. There is help there. Please do not give up.

Dartmouth, I saw a woman leaning in a doorway, as casually as if it was a sunny summer's day. Layers of tattered clothes hung loosely on her petite frame, and her dark lined face was upturned to the sky. *How long has she been there? Could there be two crazy people out? God forbid she is homeless.* I pulled a couple of dollars from my pocket and held them in my fist as I walked toward her. When she saw me, she offered a friendly smile. I opened my hand, but she waved the money away.

"You're Win, right?" She chuckled at my surprise in hearing her say my name and confessed, "Heard 'em call your name at that coffee place. I'm Gabriela."

"Hi. What are you doing out here?"

Her eyes twinkled as she replied, "Maybe same as you."

I thought it best not to think too much, so I turned to the obvious topic, the weather. "They say we got over 27 inches."

"You can't outrun 'em, you know?"

"Who?" I asked glancing around.

"The demons." I deliberately did not react. "I saw you running. No one runs like that 'less it's from them."

"Is that right?"

"It is. They love the weak ones. You better get some sleep."

"Easier said than done," was all I offered. I was reluctant to acknowledge that she might know something about me.

"Know what you should do?" I shook my head. "Stand on the Bible...like this."

"Stand on the bible!? What?"

Not another soul was in sight, but she lowered her voice. "It works. Stand like this...with your palm up." She posed and the flurries cast an angelic light around her. "Your mother is passed, isn't she?"

"She is," I admitted suspiciously because she could not have overheard that in any coffee shop.

"That makes a woman more vulnerable, more..."

"Well, she died a long time ago..."

"I know. She did it herself, right?"

I nodded and asked myself, *How could she possibly know that? Spooky.* Curiosity kept me there. Gabriela let out a blood-curdling scream. I decided indeed, *there are two crazy people in the streets.* Her scream echoed back through the urban canyon.

"That is the sound of loneliness."

"How do you figure?"

"Cuz it reminds you that no one else is around to reply. Just you, ya know?" I blinked a few times to see if she would disappear. She did not. " I'm telling you. Stand on the Bible with out hand up, so..."

"Like a lightning...?"

"Rod. Right. It will give you strength. You can save yourself." She fished a crumpled paper out of her pocket. I was too cold to read it, so I tucked it in mine. "What are those streaks of light in the clouds parting in the east?"

"What?" All I saw was the low, grey sky.

"'Night is over, and day is coming."[66] She broke off and added quickly, "I gotta go."

"Wait. Let me buy you a coffee," I suggested while I turned to dust the snow from the back of my coat. "The Plaza..." I turned. She was gone. Round I went in a circle. Not a soul. Not even footprints.

I forgot about coffee and trudged home. The sight of the remaining pills on the table reminded me I had taken them. *Must'a been hallucinating.* The snow was melting and trickling onto my eyelashes, so I stuffed my hand in my pocket for a tissue. There I found the crumpled paper Gabriela had given me. Psalm 86 was written on it. *Okay. So not hallucinating, Maybe she was a messenger from an alternative universe or something.* I decided to try the bible thing. *What's the harm, long as it doesn't attract any evil spirits?*

Before I smudged the room, I laid a crucifix on the table and placed a giant, black Bible on the floor. I stood as Gabriela had suggested, raised my hand, breathed and glanced at the psalm for the lines which I muttered. "Listen to me, Lord, for I am helpless and weak. Save me from death," *Geez, this is serious.* "Listen, Lord, to my prayer; hear my cries for help. I am in trouble. Have mercy on me; strengthen me and save me. Show me proof of your goodness. I am in trouble. Please answer me. Amen." I waited for a reply. Nothing, as I expected. With more conviction, I repeated "I am in

---

[66] Shakespeare, William, *Romeo and Juliet,* Act 3, Scene 5

trouble. Please answer me. Amen." Nothing. And then, out of no-where, a gross, stomach-churning stench filled the room, burned my eyes and choked me. The air became a dense, inky blackness. A reddish-brown man-creature with horns on his head appeared.

The taste of bile gassed onto my tongue. The creature flapped his massive wings so mightily that they launched my belongings throughout my room: mugs, plants, everything. I dodged and trembled. Magically words appeared in the hot air in front of me. I read aloud. "If you do not come in the name of Jesus Christ, go back to your source and be lifted for light." When the dark angel's wings appeared to falter ever so slightly, I repeated the words. His wings visibly weakened. I raised my voice and repeated it once more, and then continued. "Lord Jesus Christ, at the foot of your cross, I ask you to surround me with your holy light." With that, I transcended my room through a glorious, golden glow that oblit-erated all negative thoughts and feelings. Fear and confusion were replaced with a wondrous euphoria that radiated in every cell of my body, and then I vaporized. I wafted outside. From that safe distance, I peeked in. All my possessions were still crashing around. I didn't know if I was in the middle of a hallucination or a divine spiritual experience, but I prayed again and added, "Lord

Jesus Christ, if you return me to my room, could you make it so I don't have to clean up that mess?"

I can not say with any degree of certainty that any of this actually happened. If I did leave my body, I reentered it. My firm mattress was solidly under me. Once certain I was there and not in the air, I got up without turning on the light as was my habit, so I could feel my way to the bathroom and not awaken completely. I stubbed my toe on the night stand and clicked on the lamp. Woa. It appeared my last prayer had been answered. The room was more organized and tidy than ever. The remaining pills were still on the table. I slid them back into their bottle and put the bottle in the drawer. My face reflected foggily in the mirror,

so I assumed I was alive. Very sleepily, I brushed my teeth. I didn't want anymore weirdness, so I got in bed and miraculously fell into a long deep sleep.
END

Teen Suicide

I had made a previous attempt in my teens, a trying time for almost all humans. About thirty-six students, ages 15-24, attempt suicide ever day in the U.S.; eleven succeed. This group is particularly vulnerable for two reasons. The first is, as mentioned on page 37; their brains are not fully formed, in particular the prefrontal cortex, the rational section that responds with good judgment and an awareness of long-term consequences. Instead they process information with the amygdala, the emotional part of the brain. Second, their lives are rife with stress enhancers: exams, growing pains, families, alienation, bullying, alcohol and drug use, exposure to imagistic or actual violence and mental or physical abuse. They carry all these with them into the world of higher education where they face the added stress of homesickness, functioning independently and coexisting with classmates who are from vastly different cultures or have alternative ways of thinking. Anxiety is rampant among college age-students, and "between a quarter and a third meet the criteria for depression."[67] One large university claims an average of 15%, (9000) of their 60,000 students seek help in their mental health center. Nationwide, educational institutions continue to set up programs to address depression and prevent suicide. Their efforts have encouraged more sufferers to come forward and, to some degree, chipped away at the stigma, yet depression is on the rise.

***

As a young teen, around 1966, circumstances led me to be on my own in Amsterdam. A few months after my arrival, I fell under the spell of a dashing womanizer, a Dane named Mads. He was nearly twice as old as the European and American ex-pat students with

---

[67] Henriques, Gregg, *A New Unified Theory of Psychology,* 2011

whom I had become friends. Our coterie, colorfully clad females and concupiscent young men sat in cafes chatting endlessly about music, fashion or big news such as Princess Beatrix's wedding or the construction workers' riot, but eventually we always came back to our favorite topic, ourselves. We were all going our separate ways for the summer, and during our last klatch, Fenella campaigned for us to meet at her family's vacation place in Andalucia in Southern Spain and won. The sight of a convertible jaguar drew her out of her chair and sent her thick red tresses cascading down the length of her narrow back. "Mads!" He pulled along side our café table, jumped over the door and brushed his hand along his crushed purple velvet jacket. Exuding natural charisma, he fixed his incredibly blue eyes on mine, strode directly toward me and planted lingering kisses on my cheeks in greeting. "Where have you been hiding this exotic beauty," he asked, but they were too busy saying their farewells to hear or respond. "I will be back for you," he whispered before he whisked Fenella off to the airport.

I inquired about the relationship between them. Our friends waved it off as "nothing" and "a fling." Ten days later, true to his word, Mads reappeared and never left my side. Alone and far from home, I welcomed his over-attentive companionship while he basked in my juvenile adoration. We didn't go to Spain with the others, but we took a flat together and that provided a stability I had not known for a long time. I refused to allow anything to shake it, not letters from Fenella, lingering perfume on his clothes or rumors of his indiscretions. I could not believe them, only him. When I asked, he explained, "Smukke,[68] you are too young to understand. It is just flirting, nothing more."

We stayed together, and what I thought was love bloomed between us. Soon Christmas was upon the city, and heart-shaped lights hanging on the streets and outlining the canals made the damp grey streets cheerful. Around Sinterklas Dag,[69] I was shivering at the tram stop. A white-blonde sylph shined in the grey day

---

[68] Term of endearment like beautiful in Danish

[69] December 5th, Saint Nicholas' birthday in the Netherlands when children put out their wooden shoes in which he puts gifts.

and caught my eye as well as passersby; she was stunning. She was straddling her bicycle quite awkwardly to retrieve a book that had fallen from her basket. In a flash, a man swooped gallantly down and picked it up from a puddle. When he arose to return it, I saw Mads. My first thought was, *He is such a gentleman,* but it turned to *What a jerk*! when I saw him place his hand on the nape of the sylph's neck and draw her into the passionate kiss of familiar lovers. Right before my eyes, he morphed into Swarte Piet.[70] The spectacle of his infidelity was a hard slap in my face, and I realized what a naïve and trusting little fool I had been. That night when he didn't return to the flat, I pulled out the letters he had stacked neatly in his top drawer and had warned me "never to touch." On the couch, bathed in Christmas lights, I read them all. Among the many from Fenella were notes and pieces of paper with phone numbers from Saskia, Marie and I gasped, *Adeline*?! *I thought she was my friend.* The evidence confirmed my suspicions and broke my trust. I packed my belongings. The next day he showed up with flowers and a smile calling, "Smukke? Skat?[71]" I threw the letters at him and rebuked him for cheating, "and with Adeline," and "the girl on the bicycle, whoever she is." Shockingly, he calmly denied it. "No. It isn't true. You just love me too much." Confusion scrunched up my face, and he clarified. "You are too jealous." I knew I was, but then he pushed his luck. "You did not see me kiss her." *Is he really expecting me to disbelieve my own eyes?!* The argument that ensued was loud and long and senseless and ended with me quoting one of the notes, "Mads, le meilleur amant du monde. The best lover?!" His ego would not let him deny that one. For a long tense moment, we stared at each other, and then he lunged forward, grabbed me by the arms and stood in silence staring into my face before he shoved me away so forcefully that I fell backwards. Instead of helping me up, he stormed out, slamming the door behind him. That night, without a word to anyone, I left him and the Netherlands.

---

[70] A scary beast who takes naughty children away in Saint Nicholas' empty gift sacks. See page 52.
[71] Sweetie in Danish

At home in the States, I settled into an apartment near the Boston Public Garden. Because I had long been estranged from my American life, I had no one there to contact, and I couldn't bring myself to call my friends in Amsterdam, admit to how stupid I had been. I had gushed on and on about how "I met my prince." Being so alone allowed the scene with Mads to play over and over, and I actually began to question whether I had seen him kiss the sylph on the bike. *Had I made a mistake? Had jealousy driven me to walk out on my true love, my place, my friends, my life!? What did I do?* The dark winter days invited the black dog. He followed me through my every lonely waking hour and imbued me with a superb exhaustion that ached in my muscles and bones. I felt like a last autumn leaf on a vast field of snow that stretched to the horizon. One afternoon, I tidied my apartment, took a shower, did my hair and touched up my nails. In the light of my candles, I smudged the room, and offered a native prayer to the Great Spirit. I sat at the table and one by one began to swallow two handfuls of sleeping pills. *I want to go to sleep and not wake up tomorrow.* "To die, to sleep. To sleep, perchance to dream—ay, there's the rub, for in that sleep of death what dreams may come..."[72]

I thought I had succumbed to the pills, so I was disappointed and annoyed at the roar of an enormous furnace. That meant I was still alive, and I would have to continue to deal with life. I gasped, *Or have I gone to Hell?!* I glanced around and saw I was not in my bed but high above, eye level with the ornate crown molding. *Perhaps I had succeeded and I will be what? Stuck in this room forever?* The room smoldered in an orange firelight, and giant flames lapped at the walls. *This IS HELL!* Panting in the screaming heat forced me to suck in a disgusting odor like the spray of a surfeit of skunks. Flames lapped the entire height of the fourteen foot ceilings. *Wait. Maybe there a fire?* A sea of wax that had melted at the base of the tapers was ablaze; the curtains, the table, everything was ablaze. I squinted and saw a girl on my bed below, who upon a closer look, I realized was me. In a moment,

---

[72] *Hamlet* Act 3 Scene , Shakespeare, William, circa 1599-1603

we were one, and I tumbled to the floor. I moved my hand right into a puddle of vomit. Though my head felt as heavy as a pile of bricks, I managed to raise it, got to my feet and grabbed the small fire extinguisher. It was useless against the inferno. Firemen banged mightily on the door with their fists, and I called out weakly, "Help. Help." As I watched their ax blades bust through the door, questions and thoughts ran through my head. *What is going on? Am I dying? Am I dead? I can't be. I don't want to die! I don't want to die, at least not if I have to go to Hell.* Everything went dark

END

There are indeed many suffering from unbearably painful terminal illnesses who want to die, but those suffering from MDD do not. Some plan with deliberation and still others do it in a blinding flash, but that is not really what they want. For this reason it is necessary that the society become more open about integrating people who are sad or depressed, and for the depressed to make every effort to be among people.

After the attempt, I did just that. I returned to Europe, at least to be with my friends, but the depression remained.

After the attempt during the lawsuit, I was much older. I became much more proactive. I read, went to groups and found a therapist. I am still in touch with him. It was, and has been quite an educational, enriching and helpful experience.

Therapists

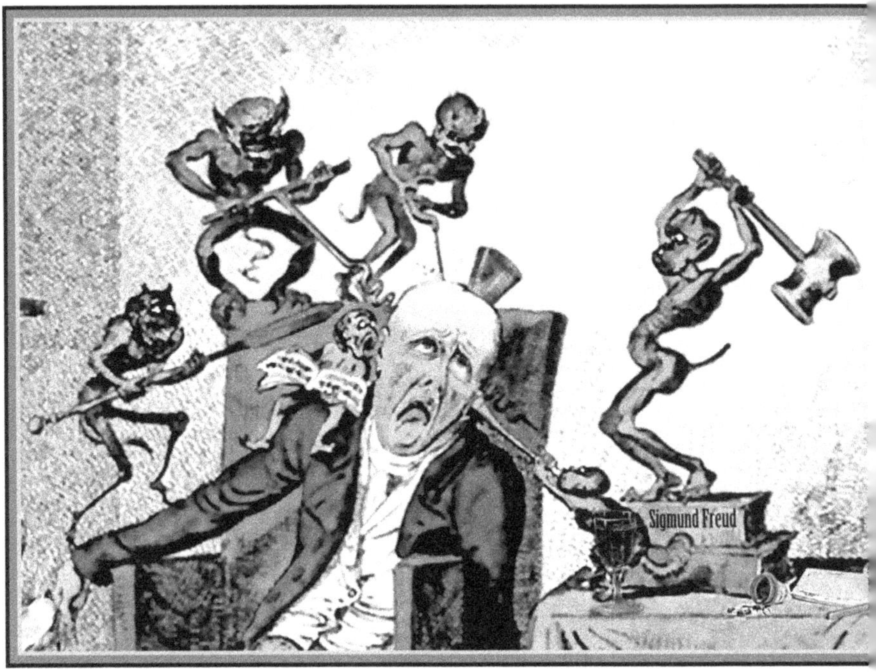
Sigmund Freud

✿6. Therapists, Finding One, It takes time.

As aforementioned, medication can alleviate the symptoms of depression that interfere with daily life, but it does not find the urchins responsible for it. Once again, while many people experience mild depression or are blue for a couple of days, Major Depressive Disorder is different. MDD is being down for weeks or months with a sense of worthlessness, extreme fatigue, the inability to concentrate, sleep, stay awake (insomnia or hypersomnia), find enjoyment in anything, (anhedonia) and or recurring thoughts of suicide. Four or five of the symptoms amount to an MDD diagnosis. Two of the most popular treatments, among the many therapies available, are Cognitive Behavioral Therapy (CBT) developed by Dr. Aaron Beck and insight-oriented therapy, Psychodynamic (PD) based in Sigmund Freud's psychoanalysis.

CBT is a thought/behavior approach to dealing with concerns that are clearly defined and affecting patients' lives; for example, anger, substance abuse, phobias and mild depression. Very simply stated, CBT involves a patient, or client as some prefer, working on a particular problem with a therapist over a 16-20 week period. During that time, they examine patients' perspectives on the problem, identify negative thinking and recondition sufferers to think more positively.[73] And this can be helpful to some; however, often, those with MDD have no idea about the source of their symptoms. In response to emotional or physical trauma, the brain can block the memory. PD therapy engages the patient in exploratory conversations that may excavate blocked information buried deep in the unconscious or, according to some therapists, in past lives, or they may find there are things best left alone. In order for patients to locate the urchins, the traumatic events,[74] and then share them, a deep trust with the therapist is essential. The first step is finding a psychiatrist whose specialty and person-

---

[73] Explained further on page 152.
[74] Such as rape, physical abuse, car accidents or other

ality are compatible with the patient's own. This process, combined with hours of talk therapy, is time consuming and costly for insurance companies. As a result, despite the data proving PD more effective for MDD, they may only offer to pay for CBT. However, if it does not work, they should allow a referral to a PD therapist.

***

To see a psychiatrist, a specialist, I needed a referral from my general practitioner. As always, he was booked into the next season. When I impressed the urgency on the scheduler, her markedly blasé retort was, "If you are in distress and need immediate intervention, you should go to the emergency room." *Again, the emergency room, and now "intervention."* When did "intervention" replace the word care? (Doctors and hospitals have their own language that distances them from patients.) Once I received the requisite referral. I embarked on the daunting task of finding a psychiatrist with whom I could connect from the list provided based solely on name, gender, location and specialty. It included quite a few psychologists and counselors who usually have PhD's or Masters. However, I preferred one with a medical degree and a prescription pad, an experienced psychiatrist. At that time, I was not sure exactly what my problem was. I mustered my courage and called, but I was discouraged by the recorded messages. One was, "the doctor is not taking any new patients." I revisited the list, but found no one. Months passed, and then I tried again.

The Therapists

DR. TARDY TIPPLER: I arrived on time; she did not. For added privacy, many private psychiatrists do not have assistants which she did not. Therefore, I sat alone in a rather dingy waiting room and waited and waited. Impatience escalated to anxiety sprinkled with aggravation, but it had been three weeks since I made the appointment. Forty minutes later, she sauntered in with a giddy grin and a flashy boutique shopping bag; no apology. Giddily she announced she had had "a lovely lunch," held up her index finger and told me to, "Hold on while I get settled." Following the rustling of bags, she invited me in. She gushed on about her meal of salmon mousse and pinot grigio of which her demeanor suggested she had had several glasses. Her tardiness shortened our session so much there was no chance for me to say much, not that I was inclined to share. She suggested we find another time. We did, but I had no intention of returning.

NEXT!

DR. NUBEE: In a voice so shy it was just above a whisper, she introduced herself. "I am Doctor Nubee, and I am here to help." She focused on my intake sheet and jotted copious notes in tiny handwriting on the yellow pad balanced on her knees covered by a plaid skirt. She had such a fresh young face; I guessed her degree to be brand new. Her straight, blonde hair was cut in a pageboy that swung over the shoulders of her beige, buttoned up cardigan. Her shoes remained flat on the floor while she absent-mindedly toyed with her strand of pearls, and she asked me questions that included, "Who is the president of the United States?" "If you could be any animal, what would you be?" She wrote my every word. I interrupted her. "Is this going to be the whole session?" She blushed and stammered, "Let's just get through this." After my last reply, she went into the adjoining room inadvertently leaving the door ajar. I watched her leafing through one of the gigantic diagnostic criteria books to compare her notes to passages therein. She returned, sat exactly as before and delivered her diagnosis. I asked, "What's next?" she excused herself and left. She was gone so long, I went home. I never heard from her again.

NEXT!

DR. CELEBRITY: He was out of my insurance network. Beyond the first free consultation, it was a whopping $300 per session out-of-pocket. I knew I couldn't afford him, but I was curious and had the insane, fleeting thought that maybe I was so messed up he would see me for a cut rate. He had a pre-intake form, for he had to approve one worthy of his expertise. "State, as briefly as possible, your reasons for seeking therapy." *Let's see: unrelenting thoughts of suicide, dissociative episodes, and I have recently become enamored with vintage Purdey shotguns.* I had no intention of using it on myself. I was, and am, fascinated by the paradox of a weapon, used to kill animals, adorned with rose scroll or a graceful creature. I figured mentioning it might get me in. Something did; a few days later, I was in his office that looked like one of the rooms in a Newport mansion. Over-sized gold embossed books were displayed on his desk. A Rothko painting hung on the wall by a marble statue of a Greek god; plush silk carpets were underfoot, and I was pretty sure I had seen the silver pitcher at one of Skinner's[75] auctions. *Was I supposed to bring a financial report?* My thoughts were interrupted when he strode in. He nodded his head in greeting, draped himself in the leather armchair and crossed his legs like a European. I was dumbstruck. The thumbnail photo posted by his online bio did not do him justice. He was a dead ringer for Cary Grant. In a God-given, honeyed voice that belied his ruggedness and years, he complimented my Chanel blouse and asked if I would "like something to drink?" I nodded, "Coffee," and he placed an order over the phone. *He has such lustrous hair.* Post haste the beverages were delivered on a cart by a woman in a proper, navy blue maid's uniform. We did not discuss me but favorite haunts in Paris, Amsterdam and Rome. I left feeling as if I had been on a first date. With dismay and relief, I read his email that came that evening, "Pursuant to our consultation, I have decided, this practice is not the best match at this time."

NEXT!

DOCTOR, MR. ROGERS:[76] The tall slim, salt-and pepper haired man entered the room with a gentle smile, removed his

---

[75] An auction house in Boston, Massachusetts.
[76] Fred Rogers (1928-2004) Presbyterian minister and American icon of children's educational entertainment known for his peaceful and earnest connection with his young audience.

jacket and slipped on a cardigan. The theme song to the children's TV show, "Mr. Rogers" played in my head. "It's a beautiful day in the neighborhood.[77]" Very gently, he apologized, for he had been incorrectly listed on the PD[78] therapy list, and was actually a CBT[79] "guy. "Based on your intake form, I don't think CBT is for you." I knew that, but I was willing to try CBT with this kind man because the daily war against thoughts of worthlessness and ending my life was exhausting me. I mentioned it. He nodded in understanding. "With certain depressions, suicidal ideation is a serious problem. If you like, we can talk for a while." We did, and I left with a referral to a psychopharachologist for medication, "to tide you over." As a psychiatrist, he could have written a script, but because I was not his patient, he had to refer me.

NEXT!

THE PSYCHO-PHARMACOLOGIST: He was a pale, bony man in a white lab coat who sat engrossed in writing. Without racing his head, he used his free hand to motion me to a chair. The air felt cooler in his office than it did in the hall. He shifted his attention to a note, took a good long moment to read it and turned back to his writing asking flatly, "So you are depressed. Right?" So far, I had not had a definitive diagnosis, so I replied, "I am not sure. I think so." While he read notes on his computer, I imagined his upbringing to have been in a nice, suburban home with two repressed parents, a younger sibling and two Golden Labradors. I also gathered *he missed all the empathy-awareness programs.* Doctors take those to counter the detached dispositions they acquire during clinical training. He confirmed my name and date of birth, scratched the prescription on the pad, handed it to me and muttered, "This should do the trick. Takes time to work. Come back on the..."—he flipped through his daily planner and gave me

---

[77] Theme songs for the children's show *Mr. Rogers Neighborhood*.
[78] Psychodynamic Therapy, number of sessions dictated by need, is aimed at providing insight into one's past to achieve greater understanding of self.
[79] Cognitive Behavioral Therapy.

a date apparently unconcerned if it was good for me. At home, I looked up the medication. I filled the script. I didn't take it.

NEXT!

DR. PERFECT. The sixth doctor was an ancient man. His office looked as though he had taken it over from Dr. Sigmund Freud himself. Slats of sunlight dappled the tapestry draped over the couch, dusty books filled the shelves between small sculptures used as book ends and stood in stacks on the floor. Beneath his shock of cotton white hair, his eyes twinkled with kindness. His loving heart had long ago slipped a permanent smile across his lips. An air of wisdom and calm emanated from him whether he was listening or talking which he did in soothing tones. He waved off any notions I had about being "mentally ill," and insisted I was "a survivor," that it was unresolved issues, the urchins ages old, were interfering with my ability to interpret the world accurately. He validated the pounding stress that raged on though the lawsuit had ended it. "Of course you are distraught. If someone whips you, you have every right to cry. But killing yourself? That does not accomplish anything. Ask the people who have done it." I laughed, something I never expected to do in therapy. Tragically for both of us, our fourth session was our last. Dr. Perfect died. An immense sense of guilt and abandonment came over me. Then I heard Wayne Dyer say, "Change the way you look at things, and the things you look at will change."[80] Rather than viewing my good-hearted doctor's death as a problem for me, I accepted him as proof that a therapist who devotes his life to helping people does, in fact, exist. It was a blessing that I had met him. RIP. There must be another.

I took stock of those with whom I had met so far and decided, I want a shrink who practices PD, has good communication skills, the ability to express empathy, a genuine kindness about him/her, one who believes medication alone is not a cure and lastly, if possible, has no annoying intake questionnaire.[81]

---

[80] Dyer, Wayne. "The Power of Intention," Hay House, Carlsbad, CA, 2010.
[81] The questions represented here are those I recall from many I filled out over the years. See page 287.

Notes/Thoughts:

ONE:

The intake process shouted to me that I was not in a place of care but of scientific study. But it is what it is, and I wanted something from it. I told myself to try to "keep calm and carry on."

TWO:

Insurance wasn't going to cover much. I would have to pay a little more out-of-pocket; my mind is one of my most valuable assets, your mind.

THREE:

Taking action does not mean you can change things right away.

The journey to find the proper therapy is a walking marathon, not a sprint.

Until I find the right person, have to use the tools available, books and self-help groups. People everywhere are trying to get through another day. No matter what the problem, there seems to be a group for it, anxiety, brain trauma, alcohol abuse, depression....

***

Getting to Group

Vlaki

The universe, God, a person or even a dog can intervene and redirects a person's path at any moment. My friend Slade and I have known each other for decades, and we discuss *almost* everything. Beyond the knowledge that both our mothers had chosen to end their lives, we know nothing of each other's pasts. We keep those to ourselves, and in that way, we enjoy our times together.

We had both been looking for therapists, so when we got together we shared notes. One day I noticed Slade seemed less anxious. I accused him of having secretly found a shrink and holding out on me.

"I thought you were going to tell me if you found someone and get a referral for me." Our thinking was that a cool shrink would know others like himself, but we didn't want to see the same one.

"I didn't find a shrink."

"What then? Weed?"

"Naw. That just makes me hungry. I've been sitting in on a

group. It's in a church basement. You should hear the shit people go through, how they deal..."

"What people."

"I don't know. It's anonymous. And it doesn't cost anything. I'll give you the info, but find your own group," he ordered sternly.

"Sure, but... first I need to know more.

I couldn't fathom how sitting in a room filled with the troubled wreckage of humanity would help me, so I didn't bother. The next night, incessant barking drew me to the window. In the streetlight, a black and white poodle limped in a circle and then stretched out on the sidewalk. Passersby glanced at him; no one stopped. Nothing tugs at my heartstrings more than an animal in distress. I assured myself his owners were near, getting their car or something. I returned to my reading, and then ordered a Greek salad from Niko in the restaurant downstairs. When I went to collect it, the poodle was still there. *Who would leave him for so long?* Thinking the dog might be hungry, I had Niko add a bit of souvlaki to my meal. As I knelt beside him, I saw a small puddle of blood pooled beneath one of his paws. That injury was all that was keeping him in place. He didn't have a collar or a leash. An old lady inching by with a walker on tennis balls snapped at me, "Well it's about time. Shame on you." I smiled and lured him to my place with bits souvlaki. My neighbor, Raisa, a nurse, was returning from work and noticed his bloody paw print. "What happened? Let me see." Inside, she searched his paw and found a small shard of glass. Other than a little whimper, he didn't respond when she removed it and bandaged his foot, so "nothing else will get in there until it heals." With a kiss for him and a hug for me, she went home. I tested my furry friend's ability to sit, turn around, lie down or stay on command. He was too focused on the souvlaki to do any of them, so I called him Vlaki.

In no time at all, his paw healed. He had grown comfortable in my place and followed me everywhere dragging along a little checkered pillow case. Having a stray forced me out of the house for walks and to put up found-dog flyers. His adorable mug pleased and saddened me. I wished I could keep him, but my lease had a no dogs' clause, so soon he would have to go to the pound. In the park, adorable Vlaki was a magnet for kids who came to pet him as he sat beside me on the bench. In bed at night, he lay across my feet. On the ninth day, I decided placing him in a shelter was out of the question. Instead, I thought to broaden the search for his family by placing an ad in the paper. While I sat drafting it, he charged to the door and clawed at it.

"Segen[82]?" I heard in a sweet voice from the other side, and he yipped.

As soon as I opened it, he scrambled to the young couple standing there. Love threw the young woman's arms around Vlaki and gratitude threw the man's around me.

"Thank you. Our friend was taking care of him, and he jumped to chase a squirrel...."

"From the car window," the woman added. "Some children told us you have him. Thank you. Thank you so much, she gushed.

"No problem. I didn't know your name was Segen," I told Vlaki.

"Means blessing in English," the woman bubbled, and noted they were "double-parked."

"You really should have a collar..."

"We got a new one," she said and slipped it around his neck.

Segen broke away from her, bounded back into the apartment and emerged with his checkered pillow case. We all laughed. The woman tried to take it, but I told her he could keep it as a souvenir. The man pulled out his wallet, but I refused any reward. I was happy to see Vlaki-Segen leave with his loving owners. Late that night his absence unleashed the urchins. They moved in my brain preventing me from sleeping or thinking clearly. I still had no therapist. I had to do something.

After searching self-help groups, I found one to be held in a hospital conference room. I went. Anxiety over the unfamiliar setting paced me up and down the hall. Then a flash of one of our Native Indian talking circles came to me. Sage smudge mingled with the scent of summer grass and the aroma of succotash.[83]

---

[82] Blessing in German.

[83] Derived from the Natick word msickquatash meaning boiled corn, succotash refers to a Native Indian soup. Northeast Woodlands peoples prepared it from locally available squash, corn and common beans and spring water.

Omi, one of the elders, was in the corner tending to the food. Her friends' sweet, gentle voices beckoned her. "Máttapsh Omi."

Cree Woman with a Smudge Fan.

She joined the circle. We cleansed ourselves with the sage smoke and settled down. A woman took the feather signifying she had the floor, adjusted her shawl and released what troubled her into the air. Outside, the birds sang, little girls laughed and the drummers warmed up, while whoever among the women had something to say shared. After the last had spoken, we would join hands. The memory was so strong, I could almost feel their touch. I wished I could be with them, but they were far away. One elder had always quoted Lone Man.[84]

---

[84] Lone Man (Isna-la-wica), a Teton Sioux born in 1850, fought at the Little Big Horn in 1876, died in April 1918.

"In any great undertaking it is not enough for a man to depend simply upon himself."

Wow. At that moment in the hallway in front of the hospital conference room, those words made more sense than ever. It is misguided and arrogant for any one to think she can confront all of life's challenges on her own.

I went in. The meeting buzzed with fluorescent lights and nervous tension. On one side, there was a table with coffee and donuts. Several boxes of tissues were within reach of the attendees, mostly women. They sat around a long, banquet-length table that held boxes of tissues, a small vase with dandelions and what appeared to be place cards with various slogans written in pen and marker.

Easy Does It—First Things First—
Live And Let Live—
But for the Grace of God—
Let Go & Let God—
This too Shall pass—
One Day At A Time

A man identified himself as the facilitator, gave his spiel and welcomed "newcomers." Those who had anything to share, how they were feeling or how they were coping with life did. "Hi. My name is Bob and....." As the meetings are anonymous, no last names are given, and often the first names are made up, Physically, I stayed for the whole hour, but mentally, I came and went. Going to the group had gotten me out of my apartment, but I was uncomfortable with the dark energy and unfamiliar scenario.

That night, the urchins dug up horrible memories, so I decided to try a different group. The next one was in Cambridge. The setting was similar, but the people were different, and it seemed somehow lighter. After the introductory process, a woman recited a story as complex and dysfunctional as mine. At first, I was relieved; I was not the only one who had had such a punishing background. Her tale roused the urchins buried in my mind. They stabbed me with a dose of paranoia. Absurdly, I concluded Slade had planted the woman there to mock me or investigate whether I mentioned him. The urchins are capable of disrupting all logic. However, I regained mine and realized that was ridiculous. I liked the atmosphere, the attendees and the process. No one comments or advises another. No one there is a shrink or a counselor. Each realizes she is not in a position to tell anyone anything other than her own circumstances and how she is coping and getting through her day.

ONE:

Do not share private therapy talk, not even with family and friends. They DO NOT have to know everything.

TWO:

Being proactive doesn't mean things will happen right away. Complexities in diagnoses and treatment take time to sort out.

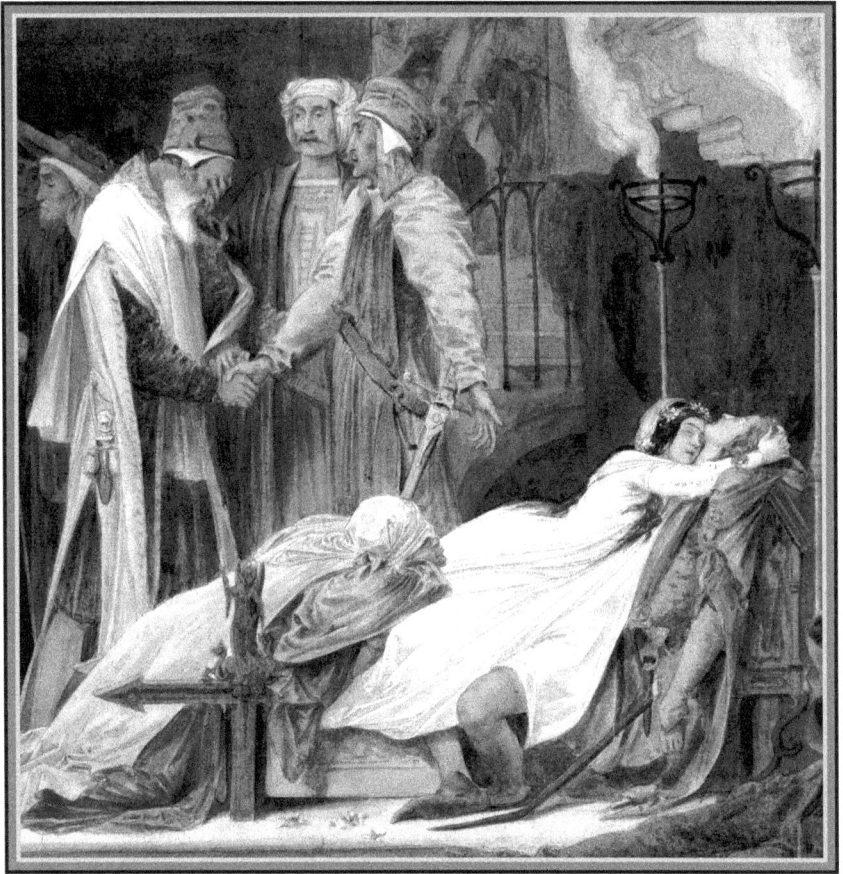

⚘ 7. Why?
⚘ Letters and Lives

Depressives and survivors can learn to cope with their agony or grief by reading, participating in groups, interacting with a therapist, taking medication or any combination thereof. Any or all are highly recommended to help prevent depressives from becoming attempters or victims. The latter leave survivors, almost guaranteed, to be deeply troubled or traumatized. In the aftermath, they run the arduous gamut of emotions: shock, grief, anger and the guilt that often accompanies suicide. Also, they are left to face the idea that personal freedom, the freedom to choose is a myth because certainly a person would not choose to kill himself. Why would he? They may recall the victim, "seemed all right the last time I saw him," which is at odds with his suicide. Survivors try to make sense of it, to find logical reasons.

First, survivors look at themselves, and those close to the victim, a spouse, partner, sibling or friend. Had one of them said or done something to cause the suicide? Unlikely. Second, survivors point to alcohol or drugs which are, in fact linked to 50% of all suicides.[85] Ethyl alcohol, (the intoxicating agent in beer, wine and liquor), opiates, benzodiazepines, and barbiturates are known depressants. Cocaine, amphetamine and dextroamphetamine are stimulants, but depression is one of the side effects experienced as they wear off. Their toxic effects manipulate the neurotransmitters responsible for mood and judgment; thus, they can be influential in exacerbating an existing depression. It is difficult to know if substances depressed the victim or if s/he was already depressed and using substances to anesthetize its pain or block out other symptoms. If overused, there is a high probability they played a role in the deadly decision. Third, survivors consider circumstances in the victim's life: physical trauma, economic challenges or emotional stressors such as financial or marital difficulties. These too are very possible contributors to depression,

---

[85] http://www.ncbi.nlm.nih.gov/pubmed/1932152

though many people grapple with them without ending their lives. The question remains. Why?

One answer is pain or what suicidologist, Dr. Edwin Shneidman, calls psychache," an unbearable psychological pain. He claims, it "stems from the thwarted or distorted psychological needs[86]" and is so agonizing and inexorable that it compels the sufferer to seek relief in death. Survivors with whom I have shared Dr. Shneidman's theory either dismiss it as "psychobabble" or nod in understanding, but none are completely satisfied with the explanation. They want pat answers, the kind given to the families of victims who passed away from terminal illnesses or accidents. "His heart gave out," or "She died instantly from the impact." These are expected explanations for familiar tragedies that bring closure to survivors and that may be repeated to anyone who asks, "What happened?" Whereas, no one is prepared to accept "He killed himself because he had an excruciating headache from depression." This is particularly difficult for survivors to accept if they have never experience depression.

One last place they look is in the victims' final words, their notes, left by less than 30% of victims.[87] Authored by those who are deeply depressed, delusional, suffering from psychache, intoxicated or high and about to kill themselves, the information provided is all but useless as a credible explanation. Usually their final words are cryptic emotional outpourings, last minute instructions for survivors or unintended riddles that leave them flummoxed, scratching their heads, forever wondering. I excavated a couple left by friends to use as examples, but the sight of my friends' handwriting resurrected long-buried grief. Thus I used the following few from artists, who studies reveal, are more prone to MDD. Writers in particular are "121%" more vulnerable to the disorder and "nearly 50% more likely to commit suicide than the general population."[88] (Yikes. Maybe I should have studied the piano.)

---

[86] Dr. Edwin S. Shneidman, "The Suicidal Mind," 1998.

[87] "Providing Access to Help," (2011). *PATH Training Manual*. Bloomington

[88] Kyaga S, Landén et al, "Mental illness, suicide and creativity: 40-year prospective total population study," J Psychiatric Res 2013 Jan; 47 (1):83-90.

❀ Letters ❀

Author, Jerzy Kosiński: May 3, 1991. (Age 58)

"I'm going to put myself to sleep now for a bit longer than usual. Call the time eternity."

Cause of death: Overdose and suffocation.

Inventor, George Eastman: March 14, 1932. (Age 78)

"To my friends: My work is done Why wait? GE."

Cause of death: self-inflicted gunshot wound.

Actor, Clara Blandick,[89] April 15, 1962. (Age 86)

"I am now about to make the great adventure. I cannot endure this agonizing pain any longer. It is all over my body. Neither can I face the impending blindness. I pray the Lord my soul to take. Amen."

Cause of death: Overdose

Musician and poet, Kurt Cobain: April 5, 1994 (age 27)

---

[89] Auntie Em" in *The Wizard of Oz*

#1.   "Thank you all from the pit of my burning, nauseous stomach for your letters and concern during the past years. I'm too much of an erratic, moody baby! I don't have the passion anymore, and so remember, it's better to burn out than to fade away.

#2.   Frances and Courtney, I'll be at your altar. Please keep going Courtney, for Frances. For her life, which will be so much happier without me. I love you, I love you!"

Cause of death: Overdose

❀ *Lives* ❀

How do the rest of victims' lives factor into MDD? Let's look.

❀

Comedian, Freddie Prinze, b. Frederick Karl Pruetzel January 28, 1977. (Age 22) (Final words.)

 "I can't take it any more. I must end it. There's no hope left. I'll be at peace. No one had anything to do with this. My decision totally.

Cause of death: self-inflicted gunshot wound.

Freddie Prinze, was a comedian leading a dreamed-of life of success in the spotlight. Available accounts suggest he came from an intact family in New York, a German immigrant father and Puerto Rican mother. At 19, he was invited to the "Johnny Carson Show" where his brilliant performance guaranteed his rise to stardom. All too soon, he was married and had a baby boy. In 1977, he had the honor of performing at the inaugural ball for President Jimmy Carter, and he had landed the lead in the TV series, *Chico and the Man*. What could go wrong? His role in *Chico and the Man* had brought discrimination down upon him. Protestors felt an authentic Chicano not a Puerto Rican should play the lead. The bundles of hate mail he received would weigh on anyone's psyche, as it did his. Publically, he brushed off the criticism with his famous line, "If I can't play a Chicano because I am Puerto Rican, then God is really gonna be mad when he finds out Charlton Heston plays Moses." In addition, Freddie had gotten caught up in the 70's drug scene, drank heavily and was said to have been addicted to Quaaludes and cocaine. Publically, he seemed fine; off stage, the booze and pills were taking their toll. He had been arrested for DUI and his wife had filed for divorce. In the end, the stress of fame, addiction and the lack of support resulted in the utter confusion and hopelessness of his last words.

❧

SYLVIA PLATH: February 11, 1963 age 30.

"Call Dr. Horder."[90]

Sylvia Plath is an accomplished American novelist, poet and short story writer. She was also the loving mother of two, Nicholas and Frieda. Her final note is the above three words that she pinned to the baby stroller. Who can tell what it means? Was it a final cry for help or a note reminding her husband to contact her psychiatrist? What could drive a beautiful and gifted young mother of two small children to kill herself? Her genes could have predisposed her to depression or it could have been secondary trauma brought about by her father's depression or the stressful events of her life after college.

Her mother, Aurelia Plath (née Schober) was born in Boston, Massachusetts to Austrian immigrants. Her father, Otto Plath, (née Platt), a medical doctor and professor emigrated to the U.S. in 1900. In her 1963 autobiographical novel, *The Bell Jar*, she refers to him as a man who hailed from "some manic-depressive hamlet in the black heart of Prussia." He was cold, distant and depressed, but she worshipped him. Tragically, World War I brought about a rabid anti-German hysteria in the U.S. All things German were maligned. German was not allowed in churches or in print. The

---

[90] There are stories that tell of Sylvia Plath having written a final letter that she mailed, possibly to her mother, but one has yet to materialize.

names of hospitals, towns, streets, illnesses and food were changed. German measles Sauerkraut, and hamburgers were, briefly, called "liberty measles," "liberty cabbage" "and "liberty sandwiches."[91] The entire German culture and its peoples were deemed suspicious and potentially anti-American, including

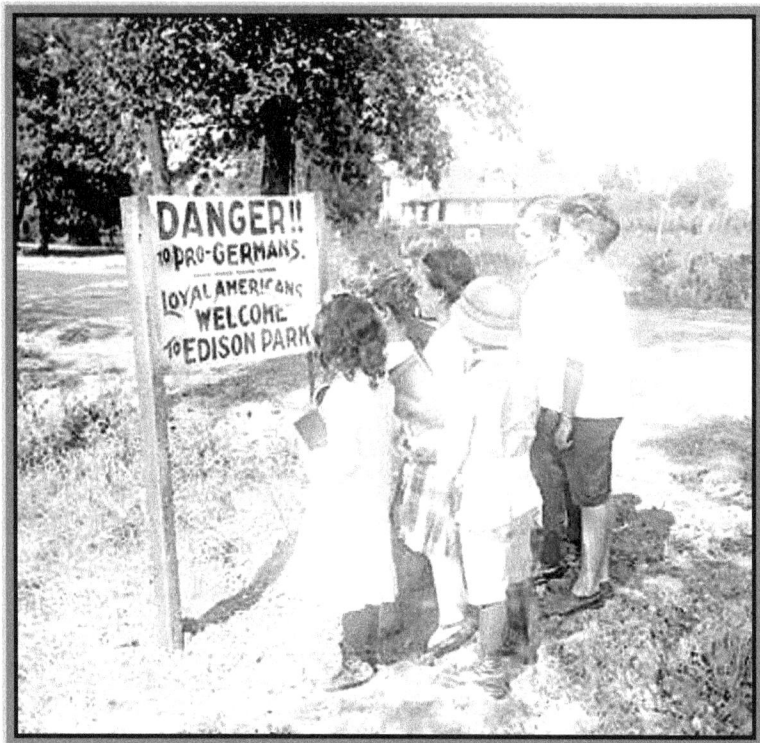

U.S. Government warning sign, 1940's

Sylvia's family. Her mother spoke German and had been stoned by children at her school while growing up. Her father was passed over for a scientific post at the University of California because he had been born in East Prussia which, along with his failure to purchase war bonds, was enough for the FBI to suspect him of being a "pro-German alien enemy."[92] Being targeted fueled his resentment toward the U. S. and added to his innate depression,

---

[91] Murrin, John M. (1998). *Liberty, Equality, Power: A History of the American People.* Harcourt Brace College. p. 784.
[92] http://www.fbi.gov/

endemic in his family. Two sisters and his mother all had "marked dark episodes"[93] requiring hospitalization. He was also physically ill with what he self-diagnosed as lung cancer. The second medical opinion he finally sought, correctly diagnosed the illness as diabetes. By then, the disease was too far along; his leg had to be amputated. Though treatment was available, he refused it, so Sylvia, a child of nine, stood by while her father subjected himself to a painful, unnecessarily early demise. Allowing himself to die was a sort of suicide, "an event from which most children never full recover, especially if the victim is a parent."[94]

A year later, a boy from her childhood reported she had cut her throat,[95] but she did not try again for 10 years. In 1953 when she was on a break from college, she left a curious note reading, "blissfully succumbed to the whirling blackness that I honestly believed was eternal oblivion,"[96] and went for a hike. Three days later she was found under her mother's front porch with a stomach full of sleeping pills. "Gravely concerned, Mrs. Plath admitted Sylvia to a psychiatric institution."[97] There she received both psychotherapy and ECT. After being released, she explained to her boyfriend Philip Mc Curdy that she had wanted to kill herself because she thought she had "lost her talent." She continued to write, graduated summa cum laude and was awarded a Fulbright Scholarship to Newnham College, Cambridge University in England. There, as expected of women of the day, she landed a man, not just *a man* but, legend has it, the most charismatic seducer on the campus, Ted Hughes.[98] He was possessed of dashing good looks and noteworthy gifts as a poet. They embarked on a three-month whirlwind romance that led to marriage. She was happy, though her diaries indicate a mild internal conflict between her career as a writer and her role as a wife. Her words are, "Make him happy: cook, play, read ... never accuse or nag - let him run,

[93] Kottler, Jeffrey, "Divine Madness," Jossey-Bass, 12/2006.
[94] The Official Sexy solitary Suicide, People with Wings, 2017 p. 16.
[95] Philip McCurdy to author Andrew Miller, *Mad Girl's Love Song*, 2013
[96] Sally Brown and Clare L. Taylor, "Plath, Sylvia (1932–1963)", *Oxford Dictionary of National Biography*, Oxford University Press, 2004.
[97] "Beautiful Smith Girl Missing at Wellesley," *Boston Globe*, 08, 25, 1953
[98] Ted Hughes was Britain's Poet Laureate from 1984 to November 28, 1998.

reap, rip - and glory in the temporary sun of his ruthless force."[99] That "force" she revealed in letters to her therapist, Ruth Barnhouse, was physical abuse. Despite her best effort, their union was tempestuous and only survived a brief five years before he left her. The piercing grief and abandonment she had experienced when her father died returned. Meanwhile Ted openly gallivanted about town with at least two women, Assia Wevil, and Susan Alliston with whom he was lying in bed the night Sylvia called and later committed suicide. She had also been in touch with her psychiatrist who wanted to institutionalize her, but overcrowding prevented it. Thus, in a winter the British call "The Great Freeze of 63," Sylvia lost her battle with psychache. Police reports state she protected her children from the gas fumes by painstakingly sealing all the cracks of the kitchen before she turned on the oven; they were not harmed.

Her father's genes and stressed behavior and her own inner conflict sent an undercurrent of suicide in the river of her short life. Its nagging thoughts are reflected in her writing. For example, in her novel, *The Bell Jar.* (Chapter 13) Sylvia, fictionalized as Esther, out for a swim with her friend Cal asks how he would kill himself. His reply, "I've often thought of that," astonishes her, and she wondered how many people had "often thought of it." That very morning, Esther had attempted to hang herself with the "silk cord" of her "mother's yellow bathrobe" because she knows she is mentally ill and does not wish to be an emotional and financial burden to her family. She fails at that attempt, then tries to drown herself to no avail.

No one knows how many times Sylvia herself had "thought of it," but she finally succeeded. In the court of public opinion, Ted Hughes is responsible. Aware of her illness, he left and had a child with his married mistress, Assia. Incredibly, in 1969, she too committed suicide with their four-year-old daughter. As the old saying goes, "Women mourn and men replace." A year and a half later, Ted remarried. Of Sylvia he said, "I was the one could have

---

[99] *The Unabridged Journals of Sylvia Plath,* Knopf Doubleday Publishing Group, 2000.

helped her, and the only one that couldn't see that she really needed it this time. No doubt where the blame lies." He is wrong. Reasons for Sylvia's depression could have been genetic or inter-generational[100] or a number of factors. They traveled forward in Sylvia's family to Nicholas, her son with Ted. He battled depression his whole life, and in 2009 took his own life. He is survived by his sister Frieda who claims not to be depressed.

❀

VIRGINIA WOOLF March 28, 1941, age 59.

Considered one of the most brilliant of British authors, Virginia Woolf was diagnosed as "mad" by her doctors. Her final "notes" to Vanessa, her sister and Leonard, her devoted husband are the most coherent and complete suicide letters I have ever read.

> "Dearest, [Vanessa]
> You can't think how I loved your letter. But I feel I have gone too far this time to come back again. I am certain now that I am going mad again. It is just as it was the first time, I am always hearing voices, and I shan't get over it now. All I want to say is that Leonard has been so astonishingly good, every day, always; I can't imagine that anyone could have done more for me than he has. We have been perfectly happy until these last few weeks, when this horror began. Will you assure him of this? I feel he has so much to do that he will go on, better without me, and you will help him. I can hardly think clearly anymore. If I could I would tell you what you and the children have meant to me. I think you know. I have fought against it, but I can't any longer.   Virginia."

> Dearest, [Leonard]
> I feel certain I am going mad again. I feel we can't go through another of those terrible times. And I shan't re-

---

[100] Depression and anxiety can be transmitted through parents' who suffer from it through their demeanor or behavior. In other words, it rubs off.

cover this time. I begin to hear voices, and I can't concentrate. So I am doing what seems the best thing to do. You have given me the greatest possible happiness. You have been in every way all that anyone could be. I don't think two people could have been happier till this terrible disease came. I can't fight any longer. I know that I am spoiling your life, that without me you could work. And you will I know. You see I can't even write this properly. I can't read. What I want to say is I owe all the happiness of my life to you. You have been entirely patient with me and incredibly good. I want to say that – everybody knows it. If anybody could have saved me it would have been you. Everything has gone from me but the certainty of your goodness. I can't go on spoiling your life any longer. I don't think two people could have been happier than we have been.   V"

Due to her complex personality, differing diagnoses have been posthumously presented: depression, mania, psychosis, schizophrenia and PTSD. Her father was prone to nervous breakdowns; Laura, her half-sister, had schizophrenia severe enough to land her in an asylum, and a cousin, James Stephen who was bipolar committed suicide. Biologically, she was a prime candidate for depression. Adding to that is a childhood of neglect and sexual abuse.[101] Without the patient present, it is difficult to state with certainty what caused her psychotic breaks, tendency to hear voices and babbling incoherently for days on end. The abuse, took place in her privileged, artistic English family; her parents, three full and four half siblings. In their home, she and her sister were raped for years beginning at ages six and eight. The perpetrators were their eighteen and twenty year-old half-brothers George and Gerald Duckworth. Virginia writes:

"There was a slab outside the dining room door for standing dishes upon. Once, when I was very small, Gerald Duckworth lifted me onto this, and as I sat there he began to explore my body, I can remember

---

[101]   Australian Institute of Family Studies, "The long-term effects of child sexual abuse," CFCA Paper No. 11 – January 2013

the feel of his hand going under my clothes; going firmly and steadily lower and lower. I remember how I hoped that he would stop; how I stiffened and wriggled as his hand approached my private parts..." [102]

In the midst of many anxiety-inducing years of sibling rape, Virginia's mother suddenly died; she had a nervous breakdown. As she was approaching the brink of recovery, her dear half-sister Stella died. These early sequential traumas rendered Virginia so psychologically fragile, that when her father then died, she had a second nervous breakdown. While regaining her strength, her brother Thoby died. In time, she overcame her grief, but her debilitating symptoms forever plagued her with racing highs, crippling lows and voices, often from birds singing in Greek. To carry on, she kept to herself and continued writing. As Lone Man said, "in any great undertaking it is not enough for a man to depend simply upon himself," and that rang particularly true for her. For her husband's constant and committed support saw her through her "madness," and no doubt, contributed to her living with the torment as long as she did. At fifty-nine, all hope and any desire to live left her, and in her own words, she had "had enough." She filled her coat pockets with stones, walked into a river, [103] and let herself drown.

❀

VINCENT VAN GOGH, March 30, 1853--July 29, 1890, Auvers-sur-Oise, France (age, 37). The post impressionist painter was an involuntary non-conformist and a bachelor for his entire short life. He exchanged hundreds of letters with Theo, his brother, friend and benefactor. Early letters reveal the nature of his feelings. In 1888, he wrote to his brother Theo: "I am unable to describe exactly what is the matter with me. Now and then there are horrible fits of anxiety, apparently without cause, or otherwise a feeling of

---

[102] Woolf, Virginia, *Moments of Being,*
[103] Panken, Shirley (1987). Acts". Virginia *Woolf and the "Lust of Creation":*
A Psychoanalytic Exploration. SUNY Press. pp. 260–262.

emptiness and fatigue in the head... at times I have attacks of melancholy and of atrocious remorse."

The letter below is not a suicide note; in fact, it is not at all clear that he took his own life. However, it is the last Van Gogh was known to have completed, and it was sent before his death.

"My dear brother,

Thanks for your letter of today and for the 50-franc note it contained.

I'd perhaps like to write to you about many things, but first the desire has passed to such a degree, then I sense the pointlessness of it. As for myself, I'm applying myself to my canvases with all my attention, I'm trying to do as well as certain painters whom I've liked and admired a great deal. I noted with pleasure that the Gauguin from Brittany that I saw was very beautiful, and it seems to me that the others he's done there must be too. Perhaps you'll see this croquis of Daubigny's garden –it's one of my most deliberate canvases – to it I'm adding a croquis of old thatched roofs and the croquis of 2 no. 30 canvases depicting immense stretches of wheat after the rain.

Hirschig asked me to ask you please to order the attached list of colours for him from the same paint store you sent me. Tasset can send them directly to him, cash on delivery, but then he would have to be given the 20%, which would be simplest. Or you'd put them into the order for me, adding the invoice or telling me how much they cost, and then he'd send you the money. Here one can't find anything good in the way of colours.

I've simplified my own order to a very bare minimum.
More soon. Look after yourself, and good luck in business.
Yours truly,
Vincent"

Vincent Van Gogh was the eldest of seven children born to Dutch parents, a "handsome" pastor and the beautiful daughter of a bookseller who was an artist. As a result, religion and art were key elements in van Gogh's family. As a child, according to his sister, Anna and their maid, he was always "aloof, and dark," with the "mannerisms of an old man" and an explosive temper which a doctor attributed to epilepsy, then a newly discovered disease. In addition, a former classmate, Calment of Arles, France, recalled Vincent had a difficult time socially. He was bullied and called names including "ugly," "very ugly," and "ungracious, impolite, sick,"[104] a description with which she agrees.

Science in the 19th century had not yet examined the affect of bullying on the neural structures allowing for changes in individuals' mood, cognition and behavior. Now evidence proves it is as damaging as physical abuse in that it too reduces the hippocampus. Thus the risk is increased for depression, anger-hostility,

---

[104] From a 1997 interview with Jeanne Calment of Arles, France, age 122, where Vincent van Gogh lived the last days of his life.

and dissociation disorders. Being perceived and accused of being odd by his family and ugly by classmates laid a foundation for depression in his life.

In his late teens, it appeared he had transgressed his inimical beginnings because he enjoyed modest measure of success in supporting himself, but his inability to control his emotions made

"Ugly" Vincent van Gog, 1866, at 13.

keeping a job difficult. He preached briefly, though not an ordained minister; becoming one was a goal he had set for himself. It was also one he sabotaged by refusing to learn the required Latin. Fortunately, the custom of several generations living together was the way of the social structure in France, and he could return home after each of his repeated failings. There, the environment was toxic due to his strained relationship with his parents who had, at least once, found his disposition troubling enough to consider putting him in an asylum. Most often, he butt heads with his domineering father who, following one of their arguments happened to die. Though a coincidence, Vincent's mother and sister, Anna blamed him and felt motivated to throw him out of the house, a rejection that devastated him.

To cope, he assumed a nomadic existence, inspired by art all alone. Unlike other men around him, he had been unable to find a love match. The first woman he pursued rebuffed him. His cousin, a widow, caught his eye, and he proposed marriage to her, but she fled in "disgust." There was some hope when he fell for Margot, a neighbor almost fifteen years his senior. Opposition from her well-to do family led her to attempt suicide.[105] Though Vincent saved her, the social pressure was too much; she moved away. Soon, destiny placed him among the Bohemian outsider set in France that included Henri Toulouse-Lautrec and Paul Gauguin. He fit right in. They shared a penchant for brothels which may have taken some of the edge off his loneliness, and they enjoyed alcohol, especially absinthe, the Green Fairy for which Vincent had already developed a taste in Antwerp to assuage his anxiety, and depression. While whiskey has a paltry 40 percent (80 proof) alcohol, Absinthe has 75 percent (144 proof). One natural ingredient, thujone allegedly has powerful effects on the brain, illuminating thoughts and heightening the senses if enough is consumed. These gentlemen were known to drink it in death-defying quantities which provided escape from their troubles but also unleashed their wild and irresponsible behavior. Vincent cut off his ear[106] during a heated row with artist Paul Gaugin; supposedly he was depressed at the time. However, it should be noted, there is no indication that either was intoxicated.

The episode brought his brother Theo to him; he had long been a source of emotional and financial support. He found Vincent a homeopathic doctor and psychiatrist, Dr. Paul Gachet who had a reputation for being kind and knowledgeable, and he specialized in treating melancholy. As an artist himself, he was said to have an innate understanding and sensitivity to creative types. Initially, Vincent reported to Theo that he "did not care for him," though he continued to see him. Over time, his opinion changed, and he wrote to his sister, Wilhelmina, Wil, "I have found a true friend in Dr. Gachet, something like another brother, so much do we resemble each other physically and also mentally."[107] Their strong relationship helped Vincent cope with his demons and Dr.

---

[105] Tralbaut, Marc Edo, *van Gogh*, 1981
[106] Reason for this are still debated, so I have not elaborated.
[107] http://www.webexhibits.org/vangogh/letter/

Gachet prescribed digitalis, once thought to remedy psychiatric ails, and Vincent continued to distract himself with his art.

Many were the days he stood painting in front of his easel among the golden wheat fields of Auvers where he was thought to have committed suicide. Now, one hundred and twenty seven years hence, that has been called into question. The most well-known historical narrative is that: One day, he walked to the field, and after painting for a while, he shot himself in the stomach. Critically wounded, he almost miraculously managed to walk the long mile back to his boarding house room. The next day, with his beloved brother Theo at his side, he died. The narrative told in 1956 bio-pic "Lust for Life" is considerably more dramatic. The reels unwind images of his painting being interrupted by an ominous murder of attacking crows. After fending them off, he collapses under a tree where he scribbles out a suicide note, shoots himself and dies. The third narrative is recently brought to the light by biographers Steven Naifeh and Gregory White Smith. After conducting extensive research of police documents of the case, they agree that, indeed, van Gogh was painting in the field, struggled back to his room and died the next day with Theo by his side. However, they disagree with the conclusion that he shot himself. Their evidence indicates someone else shot him. In other words, Vincent van Gogh's death is a case of manslaughter, not suicide.

Steven Naifeh and Gregory White Smith's interpretation is the most believable. Van Gogh's state of mind before his death and the crime scene negate suicide. His positive, future-focused correspondence with Theo suggests he was stable; an artist who had just won praise for his work and who was literally in the middle of executing a painting. While he may have been "mad," he was intelligent as the next person, and he knew shooting himself in the stomach would have been a slow and excruciatingly painful death. Furthermore, there was no gun found at the scene. For years, the biographers scrutinized the evidence:[108] police reports,

---

[108] Naifeh, Steven and Smith, Gregory White, 'Van Gogh: The Life' 12/2012, Random House Publishing, NY

accounts from neighbors, an eye witness and even a confession from a man who claims to have fired the fatal bullet. Thus they maintain van Gogh did not commit suicide.

While they may be 100% accurate, the public has not easily let go of the fossilized, romantic myth of a troubled genius who lived in an Absinthe haze and took his own life. Vincent Van Gogh's depression may have been inherited, the result of intergenerational factors, bullying, abuse or alcoholism.

Six months after he died, his brother Theo became ill and joined him at but 33. The causes listed are "dementia paralytica caused by heredity, chronic disease, overwork, sadness,"[109] but those around him, attribute his death to the loss of Vincent. Theo's wife Johanna first laid her husband to rest in his birthplace, Utrecht, but in 1914, she reburied him in the Auvers cemetery next to Vincent. A sprig of ivy from Dr. Gachet garden covers the brothers' graves in a single intertwining blanket of life.

---

[109] van der Veen, Wouter; Knapp, Peter (2010). *Van Gogh in Auvers: His Last Days*. Monacelli Press. pp. 260–264

🌸8. Depression and Nature

In the foregoing thumbnail psychological autopsies of the artists, abuse came up frequently. Science has proven it to be a major cause for depression. No one thought that. After all, the long-used biblical philosophy of "spare the rod, spoil the child" had been employed for hundreds of years and served as an effective form of discipline. The idea that it might be seriously harmful to mental health never came up. In fact, the prevention of cruelty to children became law in 1874, almost a decade after one for the prevention of cruelty to animals, and that law, as is the case with laws, did not stop it, only made it illegal and punishable. Thus most parents, teachers and other authority figures continued using it until doctors pronounced child abuse to be medically diagnosable, and states developed "mandatory reporting" laws for abuse. That means striking one "with unreasonable force resulting in injury"[110] i.e. whipping, burning or beating, not a gentle, protective swat from a protective mom to prevent a little hand from an electrical outlet. Neuropsychiatrists have found abuse, physical, sexual or psychological, including bullying to inflict physical damage on the structure and function of the brain.

Dr. Martin Teicher, Associate Professor of Psychiatry at Harvard Medical School & Director of the Developmental Biopsychiatry Research Program at McLean Hospital and his team conducted decades of research on such traumas and have found abuse to result in a constellation of brain abnormalities, particularly in the hippocampus. This seahorse-shaped region of the brain is located in the limbic system, and while small, it is vital in regulating emotional responses. "The exquisite vulnerability of the hippocampus due to the ravages of stress is one of the key translational neuroscience discoveries of the 20th century."[111] Studies reveal abuse damages the hippocam-

---

[110] Standard legal definition of abuse varies from state to state.
[111] Teicher, Martin, M.D., Ph.D, "Childhood maltreatment is associated with reduced volume in the hippocampal subfields CA3, dentate gyrus, and subiculum," E563–E572, doi: 10.1073/pnas, vol. 109 no. 9

pus by reducing its volume which puts one at risk for substance abuse and a host of other psychiatric disorders. Similarly, abandonment, neglect, maltreatment of any kind or—get this—even witnessing such treatment can permanently stunt, atrophy or inhibit healthy formation of the frontal lobe where personality is formed. Dr Teicher's "research indicates injuries inflicted to a developing mind may never heal."[112]

"Spare the Rod and Spoil the Child"

Thus the familial environment in which children spend their formative years shapes, and continues to shape, their behavior, how their brains are wired. Ideally, a home would be stable, safe, caring, supportive and filled with love, but as Ernest Hemingway writes, "families do terrible things," "make intimate harm," and "have many ways of being dangerous,"[113] as noted in the brief sketches of Plath, Woolf and van Gogh. Family therapist guru,

---

[112] Teicher, Martin, M.D., PH.D, "Wounds That Time Won't Heal," www. dana.org, October 1, 2000.
[113] Hemingway, Ernest, "A Moveable Feast," Simon & Schuster, 1964 p. 108.

Virginia Satir hypothesizes that 96% of all families are dysfunctional because two healthy parents are not present in an intact home to lavish attention and support on their children. Her idealistic model does not bode well for the millions of single-parent families in the U. S., and it gives rise to semantic debate on the meaning of "healthy." Were one to assume she is correct, almost everyone would be messed up? (Maybe we are.) And why do many siblings ask, "If home is the source of these problems, why am I alone depressed among all my siblings?"

Dr. Teicher points out, each person "has his or her own biological and psychological response to the environment." Children can be in the same family and the same house, but they are still individuals who "are different from one another—*different*."[114] For example, Sylvia Plath had a brother, Warren who lived to the ripe old age of 82 with no reported psychological ailments. Virginia Woolf was one of eight, four half and three full siblings. The latter Vanessa, Thoby and Adrian all had relatively mild mood disorders.[115] Vincent van Gogh had three brothers and three sisters. Only his favorite sister, Wilhelmina, Wil, had any mental issues. It sounds simplistic, but humans, though the same, are as unique as snowflakes. Also, though siblings have a pair of biological parents and share a common house, time between their births makes the parents and the house different. "Same" is a misconception.

Genes

So far, scientists have identified genes that predispose humans to many things: illnesses, being nocturnal or diurnal; left or right-brained; sociable or unsociable; sensitivities to taste, even color preference. Turns out, males do prefer blue and females pink.[116] They can tell how a person will react to the five modalities of

---

[114] Plomin, R. "Why are children in the same family so different from one another?" *Behavioral and Brain Sciences* (1987) 10, 1-60.

[115] Bennet M., Virginia Woolf and neuropsychiatry. Netherlands: Springer, 2013;

[116] Hurlbert /Ling, "Biological components of sex differences in color preference," *Current Biology*, V. 17, Issue 16, August 21, 2007, p. R623–R625.

taste: sweet, sour, salty, umami[117] and bitter. Those who carry the PAV form of a taste receptor perceive bitterness as intensely bitter rather than just somewhat or not at all bitter. Perhaps President George H. W. Bush who famously banned broccoli from the White House was a carrier. The length of one's alleles of the gene 5-HTTLPR,[118] determine degrees of reactivity to humor; some may burst out laughing while others only smile at the same joke. Geneticists have answers for almost everything, MDD, remains one of those riddles, wrapped in a mystery, inside a golf ball.

Solving it requires sorting though the thousands of possibilities within each of the 37 trillion human cells that make a human. To their credit, neuroscientists have located a DNA region inside of which they spied 90 genes on chromosome 3 that "appear to be related to depression..." "Humans inherit around 50% of their happiness/sadness,"[119] including bipolar/manic depression and vulnerability to MDD. "If one parent is a sufferer, a child has a 25% chance of developing some type of clinical depression. If both parents suffer, children's chances increase to 50% to 75%."[120] If neither parent is afflicted, offspring are still vulnerable, for humans are the sum total of *all* their genes which may include those passed down from historical trauma, those suffered by ancestors. A person's chances for depression can be made by observing patterns of the disorder across generations. Numerous DNA studies on descendents of veterans who suffered shell shock, indigenous peoples who were kidnapped and brutalized, African American held as slaves, victims of famines and other groups who experienced collective trauma strongly indicates the pains they felt is stored in their genes. As a result, they can be passed forward to their descendents where they provide a biological basis for susceptibility to stress and depression as with physical illnesses.

---

[117] Brothy or meaty flavor

[118] Haase, Claudia M., et al, "Short alleles, bigger smiles? The effect of 5-HTTLPR on positive emotional expressions," *Emotion*, Vol 15(4), Aug 2015, 438-448

[119] Descriptions of depression from National Institute of Mental Health

[120] Ibid.

Almost everyone knows they many of those can be inherited, for example, diabetes, arthritis, kidney and heart disease, hypothyroidism or Hereditary Hemochromatosis, HH.[121] The latter, also known as "The Celtic Curse," "Scottish or English Sickness," so called because it is prevalent among Northern European populations, stems from a particular genetic mutation that can be traced back to around 40,000 years ago.[122] Inhabitants in that area had to acclimatize to food grown in soil that, over time, had become iron-poor. Through the magic of human survival, humans adapted, so they could leech any traces of the essential mineral present in the foods they ate. As the environment changed and the mineral returned, most readapted, but in many the mutation remained, and their bodies over absorbed iron. With no where to go, it collects in the vital organs and joints causing diabetes, loss of vision, cirrhosis, acute arthritic pain, impaired memory and severe depression. Two authors, John Steinbeck IV[123] and Ernest Hemingway were diagnosed with HH, but too early on the time line for them to be treated. Doctors learned about HH in the 1800's, but the guilty gene was not identified until 1996. Hemingway had almost all the symptoms, most notably depression and excruciating pain. John Steinbeck IV inherited HH from his father, the famous author, who never displayed symptoms but was a carrier. The medical histories of our relatives and ancestors hold clues to the biological beings who we are today which underscores the importance of examining them as best we can.

---

[121] Wertheim, Bradley, "The Iron in Our Blood That Keeps and Kills Us" The Atlantic: January 10, 2013.
[122] http://www.americanhs.org/celtic.htm
[123] Son of the 1962 Nobel Prize-winning author, John Steinbeck (1902-68).

October 1818, Young Abraham Lincoln lamenting his mother's death.

9. When Depression Never Ends: Acceptance, Abraham Lincoln

If you're going through hell, keep going.

Winston Churchill

MDD plagues some sufferers from as far back as they can remember, and then life adds insult to that injury by piling on more misfortune and death. What does one do when depression never ends? Distraction is one way to cope, and it has been proven to ease anxiety, stabilize the spirit and allow one to function, or in some cases, go out and do great things. For example, William Falkner and Ernest Hemingway focused on their writing and received Nobel Prizes; Buzz Aldren, the astronaut who walked on the moon, became the chair of the Mental Health Association and began planning for space tourism; Diana Spencer, Princess of Wales turned her attention to ridding Angola and Bosnia of landmines; Prime Minister, Sir Winston Churchill led his country through its darkest hour to victory over Nazism. What about President Abraham Lincoln? Well he became the unifier of a nation and its "Great Emancipator."

Genes

According to those who knew Abraham Lincoln, his desperate sadness was as much a part of him as his height. They claim it was rooted in his early life. One of his schoolteachers, Mentor Graham, said, young Lincoln "told me he felt like committing suicide often." Friends recalled how he "wept in public and recited maudlin poetry." Joshua Speed, his closest friend, describes Lincoln's appearance when they first met. "As I looked up at him I thought then, and think now, that I never saw a sadder face." Abe's law partner wrote, "He was a sad-looking man; his melancholy dripped from him as he walked." To Robert Wilson, with whom he served in the Illinois legislature, Lincoln "was so overcome with mental depression, that he never dare carry a knife." He was a tall manifestation of clinical depression and suicidal ideation, yet somehow he survived and left a legacy of monumental accomplishment.

Trans/Intergenerational[124] Trauma

Historians and psychologists observing patterns of psychological disorder across the Lincoln generations conclude his chances for depression were high, almost predictable. It ran through the paternal side of his family. His great uncle declared to a court of law that he himself and several other of his family members were "deranged." No one would label Abe as deranged, but he was most definitely depressed and possibly suffered from PTSD. His father, Thomas, experienced early childhood trauma when his own father, President Lincoln's grandfather, and a Native American were killed right in front of his eyes. "While Abraham Lincoln" [President Lincoln's grandfather] "and his three boys, Mordecai, Josiah and Thomas," [President Lincoln's father] "were planting a cornfield on their new property, Indians attacked. Grandfather Abraham was killed instantly. Mordecai, the oldest son at fifteen, sent Josiah running to the settlement half a mile away for help while he raced to the nearby cabin. Peering out of a crack between logs, he saw an Indian sneaking out of the forest toward his eight-year-old brother, Thomas, still sitting in the field beside their father's body. Mordecai picked up a rifle, aimed for a silver pendant on the Indian's chest, and killed him before he reached the boy."[125] The horror of such an experience can not only affect the witness but be transmitted to their children.

---

[124] Transgenerational trauma includes those suffered by ancestors that go forward. Intergenerational is from parents or grandparents who are among us.
[125] Donald, David Herbert, *Lincoln.* Simon & Schuster, 12/ 20/2011

Childhood Hardship

Like many pioneer families, the Lincolns endured taxing conditions that challenged their very survival. Early in December of 1816 seven-year-old Abe, his nine-year-old sister, Sarah and their parents, Nancy and Thomas lived in Kentucky, but they were planning to relocate to their new land in Pidgeon Creek Indiana. To facilitate the move, the father built a boat to float the family there. They boarded with their few belongings, including "four hundred gallons of whisky[126]" During pioneer days, "Incredible quantities of "the fiery liquid," whisky were consumed by everybody, women, children and preachers included. Several bottles or, at the very least one was in every cabin — to offer it was the first gesture of welcome, to refuse unpardonable incivility. Whiskey served as currency and medicine, good reasons for Thomas to be certain he had ample supply. Once ashore, the family had to enter a forest that was dense and darkened by vines growing among the canopy of branches. By all appearances it seemed impenetrable, but they journeyed in on "two horses, used by the wife and children for and to carry their little equipage for camping at night....[127]" All accounts report their poverty to have been torturous and their situation primitive, even for pioneers of the day. In an effort to keep the family minimally warm, Thomas built a "half-faced camp," a three-sided shelter without a floor, windows or a door! The fourth side was left open, and there they built a fire for cooking during the day. At night, they hung a heavy animal skin over it to keep dry and prevent bears from making them a last meal before hibernation. In that single, 14-foot space, they resided through the winter and the following eleven months. Their work was double that of the average settler because their land was full of timber that had to be cleared before they could build their permanent cabin and begin farming. Once they did, they faced the back-breaking chores of harvesting and even the preparation of food. Whenever they needed flour for bread, Little

---

[126] Nicolay, John, A Short Life of Abraham Lincoln, 1902, p
[127] Nicolay, John, *Lincoln,* The Century Co., N.Y., 1904

Abe had to ride twenty-eight miles to the mill and back. Hauling water, chopping wood and hunting can be enjoyable on a weekend camping trip but physically and psychologically punishing as daily do-or-die responsibilities of a boy of eight. Had this contributed to child Abe's inexorable sadness, or was it something else?

Shame, Abuse

Every child who has less knows the pain of being heckled and demeaned by other children. Bullying shreds self-esteem, bows one's head when they walk. Abe was a strong boy who held up under that; his shame came from well-known family secrets about his parents. The first concerned his mother who Abe absolutely revered; "Angel" he called her and claimed, proudly to his friend William Herndon, "All that I am or hope ever to be I got from my mother, God bless her.[128]" He admired everything about her, how she read to him and taught him to read. The "secret" about her, which he confided in Herndon was, "My mother was a bastard, was the daughter of a nobleman, so called, of Virginia. My mother inherited his qualities and I hers."[129] Herndon kept Abe's confidence, but everyone knows everything in small towns and due to the conservative mores of the day, his mother's reputation was damaged. Another damning tale concerned her and his father. It arrived on the tongue of her nephew Dennis Hanks who openly declared Thomas Lincoln incapable of having fathered Abe because "the mumps had left Abe's father castrated,[130] with "pea-sized testicles,"[131] which he had allegedly seen. In one fell swoop he named his father impotent, Abe a bastard and his mother a whore. Behind closed doors, family and community identified a land owner, Abraham Enola as Abe's biological father. Thus far,

---

[128] *Hidden Lincoln from the Letters and Papers of William H. Herndon*, Viking Press, 1938 p139.

[129] Ibid, p.73

[130] Meaning impotent at that time.

[131] Shute, Milton. MD, Lincoln's *Emotional Life,* Dorrance & Company, Philadelphia, 1957, 193.

research of historical documents fails to support those claims. However if it was true or accepted by Thomas, it would be one explanation of his brutal treatment of Abe. Biographers have uncovered evidence of Thomas' violent physical abuse of Abe and deem it far exceeded the norm. He was literally whipped for anything Thomas disliked, even reading. While his mother had tenderly and patiently taught him, his father, an uneducated man, saw no use for it. In addition, without being consulted on his availability, Thomas would lend Abe out for labor for which Thomas, not Abe was paid, making him feel like a slave. Other than living under the same roof, he and his father had nothing in common.

Recurrent Personal Loss

On October 5, 1818, Abe's "Angel," his mother succumbed to milk disease[132] which she contracted while serving as a nurse to others who had it.[133] He was utterly devastated. The nine-year-old Abe's next chore was one of the saddest any young boy anywhere should be assigned, whittling the pegs for his mother's coffin. Life can not stop for death, especially not for demanding pioneer life, so he had no time to grieve. The farm required so much of Thomas' attention, there was none left for preparing food, hauling water, caring for the children or anything else. In need of another wife to fulfill these functions, he left to secure one who had suddenly become available when her husband died. She was a former sweetheart, Sarah Bush Johnston. While he went off to her distant town, Abe, his sister, Sarah and cousin Dennis had to fend for themselves. A year had passed and Thomas failed to return, so they concluded he had died and continued without him. When he did eventually arrive, it was with plenty of helping hands, their stepmother, Sarah and her three children. Abe's sister, Sarah mar-

---

[132] Disease caused by drinking milk from an animal that has ingested poisonous white snakeroot.

[133] *The History and Personal Recollections of Abraham Lincoln* as originally written by William h. Herndon and Jesse W. Weik

ried and moved nearby; Abe enjoyed visiting her. However, tragically, she died while delivering a stillborn child. It was "a great grief to Abe, who was waiting in anxious fear in a little smokehouse when the news came to him. He came to the door and sat down burying his face in his hands. Tears trickled through his fingers, sobs shook his frame."[134] The only people who had made his grueling life tolerable, his mother and sister were gone. He was alone with his stepmother and father whose cold, hard attitude toward him never softened. When, years, later, he visited his childhood home in Indiana he wrote a short poem.

> "My childhood home I see again,
> And gladden with the view;
> And still as mem'ries crowd my brain,
> There's sadness in it too—"

Matters of the Heart

In time, Abe's hormones eclipsed his sorrows and cast his gaze most desirously on the opposite sex. It was not quickly returned because as a swarthy man of 6' 4"—then considered too tall—with but meager means, he was not exactly a catch. Still, he tried everything and anything to get their attention even, it is rumored, riding an ox bareback. His friends all agree, he had a passion for women and for sex. "It is the harp of a thousand strings," he repeatedly told his friend Henry Whitney.[135] He satisfied his needs with "acquaintances" in brothels. Joshua Speed recounts one time when Abe asked if he knew where he could, "get some?"[136] He sent him to a lady companion with a letter of introduction, and she later told Speed of the encounter. The two "stripped off and went to bed."

---

[134]Shute, Milton. MD, *Lincoln's Emotional Life,* Dorrance & Company, Philadelphia, 1957, p. 32. Reported Captain J. W. Lamar, a neighbor.
[135] Wilson and Davis, eds., *Herndon's Informants,* Henry C. Whitney to Herndon, 23 June 1887, 617.
[136] *Hidden Lincoln from the Letters and Papers of William H. Herndon,* Viking Press, 1938, p.233

"How much do you charge?"

"Five dollars, Mr. Lincoln."

"I've only got three dollars."

"Well, I'll trust you, Mr. Lincoln, for two dollars."

"I do not wish to go on credit. I'm poor and don't know where my next dollar will come from and I cannot afford to cheat you."

Amused, she encouraged him to stay. Afterwards, he "buttoned up his pants," and offered her the three dollars. She refused saying, "Mr. Lincoln, you are the most conscientious man I ever saw."[137]

Honest Abe he was, indeed, honest in all his affairs.

He continued his quest for a suitable wife, and at twenty-five, he found her in the sweet, smart, strawberry blonde, calico-clad, country beauty, Ann Rutledge. They fell in love and were engaged. "I believe his very soul was wrapped up in that lovely girl. It was his first love – the holiest thing in life – the love that cannot die.[138]" Indeed, it did not; his love Ann did. She fell ill, possibly with Typhoid Fever, and he went to her deathbed to say farewell. Ann's sister, Nancy reported, "I can never forget how sad and broken-hearted Lincoln looked when he came out of the room from the last interview with Annie..." So moved by her death was he, that he would cry when it rained because "the rain's a fallin' on her."[139] He said, "My heart is buried in the grave with that dear girl," and "he would often go and sit by her grave and read a little pocket Testament he carried with him."[140] Twice before, he had survived the emotionally draining journey through grief's dark valley, but friends claimed this time, it deepened his melancholy and led him to a nervous breakdown.[141] His confidant, Dr. John Allen,[142] helped with the treatment of the day, talking, blood-

---

[137] *Ibid,* 1938, p.51

[138] Harvey Lee Ross, a boarder at her family's Rutledge Inn.

[139] Files of the Lincoln Financial Foundation Collection, 1889.

[140] Harvey Lee Ross, The Early Pioneers and Pioneer Events of the State of Illinois, p. 101

[141] Stress induced depression that prevents day-to-day functioning.

[142] Files of the Lincoln Financial Foundation Collection, 1861.

letting, purging, starving and blue mass tablets.[143] Two years later, he had recovered, at least to his former sad self, and relocated to Springfield, Sangamon County, Illinois. He stood out as the self-conscious country bumpkin bachelor that he was. His status as a new attorney and member of the House of Representatives elevated his appeal to the opposite sex, for while he was humorous and gregarious among men, he was shy and uneasy around women who were in the majority by 24%.[144] Matilda Edwards of Illinois and Mary Todd of Kentucky held a preponderance of the men's attention. Matilda was a socialite who at

Ann, Abe and his dog, Fido

---

[143] Mercury, a neurotoxin.

[144] Kenneth J. Winkle, The Young Eagle: The Rise of Abraham Lincoln (Dallas: Taylor, 2001), 62.

but sixteen[145] had a reputation as a heartbreaker. She was a stunning beauty, tall and graceful with a conciliatory manner. Mary, twenty-three, was a Kentuckian from a prosperous family, short and pleasingly plump with an allure of entertaining geniality and a sharp wit. That season Matilda received over twenty proposals, thirty-three-year-old Lincoln's among them. Though she rather roundly rejected Abe, he held onto hope for a while. Then, for reasons only he will ever know, he went against his heart and proposed to Mary, who ostensibly had been courting him. When her acceptance failed to override his yearnings for Matilda, he confessed to those he knew, "It would kill me to marry Mary."[146] He broke their engagement, and the grave dishonor of his act broke him. This combined with the stress of his political career, led him to a second nervous breakdown or, as one woman said, to "within an inch of being a lunatic for life."[147]

Resilience was one of his strengths. He rallied and was soon reunited with his constant companion, melancholy. To regain his honor, he resurrected his proposal to Mary whom he wed immediately, by chance, in the home of his friend, Ninian Edwards, Matilda's uncle. A week after the nuptials, Abe wrote to Samuel, a friend, "Nothing new here, except my marrying which to me is a matter of profound wonder."[148] Their social circle did not consider Abe and Mary a suitable match. Reports regarding their married life vary, but something must have been right because they had four sons, Robert in 1842, Eddie in 1846, Willie in 1850 and Tad in 1853. The joy of children was not to be his for long. One by one, three of the boys died, Eddie, age four of tuberculosis; Willie age eleven of a fever and Tad age eighteen of heart failure. Together, three times over, they worked through the intense pain born of the death of a child. The grievous agony of Willie's passing was compounded by the dawn of the Civil War. Lincoln was on the verge of a third collapse, but he compartmentalized his grief by focusing on the massive task of keeping the Union together. However, from

---

[145] In the 1800's, women married at 19, but long engagements were common.

[146] Sarah Rickard, sister of Mrs. Butler, interviewed by Nellie Crandall Sanford, Kansas City Star, 10 February 1907.

[147] Jane D. Bell to Anne Bell, Springfield, 27 January 1841, copy, Lincoln files, "Wife" folder, Lincoln Memorial University, Harrogate, Tennessee

[148] Letter to Samuel D. Marshal, November 11, 1842.

time to time, the despair seeped through. For example after one the worst battles of the Civil War, he visited the front and was overwhelmed with a sense of complete hopelessness. Secretary of War, Edwin M. Stanton noted, the president had "fully made up his mind to go immediately to the Potomac River, and there end his life, as many a poor creature — but none half so miserable as he was at the time — had done before him."[49] He did no such thing. He had become familiar with his melancholy, come to accept its dark moods, and thoughts of death; he knew they would pass. He knew he had to carry on.

---

[49] *The Wichita Eagle* May 7, 1898, Kansas.

When Depression Never Ends:
Distraction, Hemingway

Ernest Hemingway and Black Dog, at Finca Vigía[150] in Cuba.

---

[150] Finca Vigía, meaning "lookout house," is Hemingway's home in Cuba, ten miles east of Havana. Ernest Hemingway Photo Collection. John F. Kennedy Presidential Library and Museum, Boston.

10. When Depression Never Ends: Distraction: Hemingway

"One of the great citizens of the world."
President John F. Kennedy, July 2, 1961

Genes/Environment

Ernest Hemingway had the same indivisible mixture of ingredients for depression as Abraham Lincoln beginning with inherited genes including diabetes and hemochromatosis (p. 97), the Celtic Curse. By 1961 when he was diagnosed, the rare blood disease, along with diabetes had already wreaked havoc on his body. His organs were seriously damaged and the resultant joint issues inflicted excruciating pain. These contributed to his already existent depression. This was not uncommon among the Hemingway family, there were six children born to mother Grace, a singer and father, Clarence, a doctor. He kept the brood in order with a heavy Congregationalist hand that often held a razor strap. Nevertheless, Ernest liked him. He was less domineering than his mother for whom he openly and loudly expressed contempt. Enter an intergenerational ingredient. Friends attributed his sentiment toward his mother to her bullying his father and clothing young Ernest in little girl's dresses, so he and his older sister appeared to be twins. She created and perpetuated the illusion until he was at least five. (She clearly had her own issues.) However, later in life, Ernest declared a greater reason for hating her, his father's death. Dr. Clarence Hemingway, some have posthumously concluded, was depressed[151] or bipolar.[152] The Hemingway

---

[151] Lynn, K. S., Hemingway. Reynolds, M., "The Young Hemingway," New York: Simon & Schuster 1987 Oxford, UK: Basil Blackwell, 1986
[152] Jamison, K. R. (1993). Touched with fire: Manic-depressive illness and the artistic temperament. New York: Simon & Schuster

children complained of the stress his "nervous condition" placed on them, and Dr. Hemingway, who had diabetes, did require repeated retreats away from the family for "rest cures." The diabetes exacerbated the attendant depression so severely that after a time, the rests were no longer effective, and he felt compelled to anesthetize his pain with a bullet from his pistol to his brain. Unfortunately, Ernest's siblings, Ursula, in her twenties, and Leicester, thirteen, were home, heard the blast and went to his room where they found him already dead. Ernest received word while en route to his home in Key West to work on "A Farewell to Arms." He was moved by the loss of his father, "the one I cared about," he wrote to his editor. He blamed his mother, "... an all time all american [sic] bitch and she would make a pack mule shoot himself; let alone poor bloody father." As aforementioned, children of victims often become victims themselves. Years later, Ursula, relieved herself of cancer-associated pain with a lethal overdose, and Leicester, who had lost his legs to diabetes, also shot himself in the head. Ernest attended his father's funeral and grieved, but he had no intention of being "a coward," like his father. As artists often do, he distracted himself from tragic reality by diving into his work. He rewrote "A Farewell to Arms" seventeen times over the next year.

Hemingway's pursuit of excellence and macho life style shaped him into the man President John F. Kennedy called, "one of the great citizens of the world." As a young man, Papa, as he later preferred to be called, set out to drink in all life had to offer. To that end, he guzzled barrels of booze, explored the four corners of the world and luxuriated in the arms of beautiful women. All are well-documented in his novels: *The Old Man and The Sea* is set in Cuba, *To Have And Have Not* in the Florida Keys, *The Garden Of Eden* in the French Riviera, *True At First Light* in Kenya, *A Moveable Feast* in Paris and *The Sun Also Rises* in Pamplona, Spain, the city that stole his thrill-seeking heart. His first visit was in July of 1923 during the rousing annual Festival of San Fermín, famous for its running of the bulls. On the Calle de la Estafeta, below his hotel balcony, throngs of revelers cheered the mozos[153] as they ran ahead of the enormous beasts thundering toward imminent death in the bullring. Along with their streams of crimson blood that had been let by glittering matadors, wine flowed in celebratory abundance, just the existential elixir Hemingway needed to keep depression at bay. He attended the annual Festival of San Fermín nine times from 1923-1959 and had made plans to again return in 1961.

Traumatic Brain Injury TBI

Other contributors to Hemingway's depression are multiple traumatic brain injuries (TBI), shellshock,[154] alcoholism, illness, and grief. Recent research has proven that individuals who suffer a TBI have a 50% chance of developing depression within the first year. As many as seven years later, those chances jump to 75%. All it takes is one to bring on symptoms: headaches, high blood pressure, blurred vision, impaired judgment and depression. Hemingway had nine or more, the most serious were:

- June, 1918: Italy, WWI, multiple injuries, concussion
- March, 1928: skylight broke on his head in Paris.
- May, 1944: back to back car accidents concussions
- June, 1945: Car overturns, knee injury and concussion
- July, 1950: Falls on the boat and suffers a concussion
- January, 1954: Plane crash in upper Nile, concussion
- January, 1954: Plane crash in Entebbe, almost deadly

His first TBI came during WWI when he was quite young, eighteen. He was an ambulance driver for the Red Cross, not a trained fighter, just a kid handing out chocolate and coffee to Italian soldiers in a dugout. When an Austrian mortar shell struck, he watched helplessly as the blast blew the legs off one man, killed two others and embedded 200 shards of shrapnel over his body.

---

[153] Those who ran with the bulls.
[154] Shell-shock is a period-specific word for Post Traumatic Stress Disorder

Despite witnessing such horror, he carried a man, unable to walk, to safety. Afterwards, Hemingway collapsed and fell into a coma, an experience he recalls as dying and coming back to life. Doctors present concur, for the description he gave of his comatose state was similar to others who claimed to have left life.

"There was one of those big noises you sometimes hear at the front. I died then. I felt my soul or something coming right out of my body, like you'd pull a silk handkerchief out of a pocket by one corner. It flew all around and then came back and went in again and I wasn't dead any more." [155]

He suffered serious wounds over his body, including his scrotum that had to rest on a special pillow[156] to recover. The remainder of his manhood was in tact, but psychologists have found such wounds trigger castration anxiety.[157] Like thousands of soldiers scraped out of the battlefields of wars, Papa had stared into the hot, dark maw of death and lived to tell. The experience itself and the wreckage of his body made him a prime candidate for Shellshock.[158] According to Dr. Earnest Jones, "Soldiers who had bayoneted men in the face developed hysterical tics in their own facial muscles. Stomach cramps seized men who had knifed their foes in the abdomen. Snipers lost their sight. Terrifying nightmares of being unable to withdraw bayonets from the enemies' bodies persisted long after the slaughter."[159] The symptoms of shellshock aka "soldier's heart" and now PTSD may arise immediately, be delayed for years or come and go. They include, but are not limited to, recurring nightmares or flashbacks, insomnia, inexplicable anger, hyper-anxiety, hyper-vigilance or sexual dysfunction. The survivors were allowed a hot shower, a good meal

---

[155] An apocryphal paraphrasing more frequently quoted than his own words Montgomery, said he used to explain the event to Guy Hickok in Italy," *The Hemingway Review* Volume 25, Number 1, Fall 2005, 112-119.

[156] The pillow is in the Hemingway Museum at Key West. .

[157] Not implying physical impotence. His wives were all reportedly happy with his amorous talents.

[158] Word formerly used for Post Traumatic Stress

[159] bbc.co.uk/history/worldwars/wwone/shellshock_01.shtml#one

and rest before being sent back on duty. The prevailing attitude was that soldiers who whined about pain or what they had seen had weak characters,[160] one of the worst insults a man of the day could receive. As a result, soldiers who had been affected tried to dismiss or deny symptoms or drown their memories and pain in alcohol, unwittingly enhancing their depressions.

Another of Hemingway's TBI occurred in Africa after a second plane accident. It "broke his skull[161]" so completely that cerebral fluid leaked visibly from his ears. Unbeknownst to him and his wife Mary, they had also crash landed on the front-page of U.S. Papers. "Hemingway and Wife Dead, No sign of life at the Wreck," was the headline, yet all present had survived.

Report from Africa: January 23, 1954

HEMINGWAY, WIFE KILLED IN AIR CRASH
'NO SIGN OF LIFE' AT WRECK . . .

The cumulative residual physical effects of these brain injuries and the flamboyant, adrenalin-fueled life of the accomplished celebrity he had become, were taxing his physical and mental well-being.

Alcohol

Hemingway was almost as famous for drinking as for writing, which he openly admitted. "I have drunk since I was fifteen, and "few things have given me more pleasure." Part of the joy he derived from drink was its ability to "make you forget all the bad," as he wrote in A *Farewell to Arms*. And he had plenty to forget, the

---

[160] Bentley, Steve, "A Short History of PTSD: From Thermopylae to Hue Soldiers Have Always Had A Disturbing Reaction To War," *Veterans of America*, January 1991 reprinted March/April 2005.
[161] Mellow, James, *A Life Without Consequences*, Da Capo Press, 1993.

war, the wounds to his scrotum and those to his heart that was broken when his love left him for another man. He always had liquor, even in the hospital, thanks to his charm and skill at finagling the sympathetic nurses. When he was released to go home to the U.S. where prohibition was in full swing, he decided to devise a way to smuggle booze with him, but he never had to put his plan into action, for the *Toronto Star* had hired him as a foreign correspondent stationed in Paris.

As a vibrant, hard-drinking American, journalist, he was easily accepted among the café camaraderie of bohemian expats known as "The Lost Generation." Among others in their ranks were James Joyce, Gertrude Stein, Sylvia Beach and F. Scott Fitzgerald, and Ezra Pound. There, in the City of Lights, in the relaxed aftermath of the war, free from prohibition, they drank and drank and drank to celebrate their creative, young lives on the continent. Fitzgerald wrote that "they drank cocktails before meals like Americans, wines and brandies like Frenchmen, beer like Germans, whiskey-and-soda like the English,"[162] and through it all, they were prolific and successful.

---

[162] Allan, Tony *Americans in Paris*. Chicago: Contemporary Books, 1977

Hemingway reported on war and politics, European society and sports, bullfighting in particular. Thus he was required to attend arenas from San Sebastian to Granada, which he did with such enthusiastic frequency that he became a noted expert. In Madrid, he deepened his friendship with the erotically charged actress Ava Gardner who accompanied him to bullfights where he educated her on bullfighting's traditions, and she picked up its dashing matadors. Once without an iota of training, he rashly charged into the bullring to confront the angry bull and was for-

Hemingway in white pants directly in front of the bull, holding the cape. 1925.

tunate enough to escape unharmed. Curious about his impulsive, free-wheeling manner, Ava asked if had ever had an analyst. He admitted "Sure I have. Portable Corona number three. That's been my analyst,"[163] and he added that he distracted his mind from

---

[163] Hotchner, A.E., *Papa Hemingway*, 1966, p 139

thoughts of killing himself by "killing animals and fish.[164] That is not to imply that he disliked animals. On the contrary, he had a well-known reputation for admiring them, even bulls. "Bullfighting is not a sport. It was never supposed to be. It is a tragedy. A very great tragedy. The tragedy is the death of the bull." [165] His appreciation for their beauty and grace, even a bull fighting for its life in the ring comes across in his writing.

"He was absolutely unbelievable. He seemed like some great prehistoric animal, absolutely deadly and absolutely vicious. And he was silent. He charged silently and with a soft, galloping rush. When he turned, he turned on his four feet like a cat...." [166]

While Papa wanted to live by the bullfighter's philosophy, that what he does is worth jeopardizing his life, he left the fighting to the matadors and settled for relishing the thrill of the contest from the stands with a bottle of booze.

Noradrenaline/Norepinephrine [167]

Papa's inherited disorder/s were compounded by intergenerational factors, TBI and alcoholism. He had devastating lows, but he also had astronomical highs from his rash thrill-seeking. Had he inherited the taste for excitement?[168] Was his recklessness related to drunkenness, delusional perceptions of his strength and talents, or was it a subconscious desire to fend off sorrow by stimulating his brain chemicals? Noradrenaline/Norepinephrine, like amphetamines, are known antidotes to depression, though only briefly, for the few moments one skis down a steep slope, wins the jackpot, whatever..... For Hemingway it was facing down a wild animal on safari; jumping into a bull ring in Spain; fishing,

---

[164] Ibid.

[165] Ibid

[166] "Bullfighting is Not a Sport – It is a Tragedy," *The Toronto Star Weekly*, Oct. 20, 1923.

[167] Noradrenaline/Norepinephrine is a chemical released from the sympathetic nervous system in response to stress, and it affects other organs in the body; therefore, it is also referred to as a stress hormone.

[168] 50% determined by hereditary genes.

in particular deep-sea fishing; covering war, despite his nearly castrating experience in WWI and boxing. In his mind, he was a boxer, though he had never trained on any level. His high opinion of his amateur skills encouraged him to challenge anyone. When heavyweight champion Jack Dempsey's sojourn took him to Paris, news of Hemingway's eagerness to fight him was in the air, but he avoided the opportunity. When a reported asked Dempsey why, he explained, he didn't think he could restrain his well honed strength and skills against "a swinging madman trying to prove something." However, another heavy weight champ and friend to Hemingway, Gene Tunney, did take him on but with kid gloves. After Hemingway had already had quite a few martinis, Tunney accepted the challenge and let Papa get in a shot or two, but, in the end, he clobbered him and his desire to take risks with professional boxers.

Instead, Papa stimulated himself, by putting into play his desire to be a double agent which, in some ways, contributed to his ghastly demise. "During World War II, he happily devoted much more of his time and energy to the field of intelligence than to his normal literary pursuits.[169] He had relationships with the intelligence section of the US embassy in Havana as well as with at least three US intelligence agencies: the Office of National Intelligence (ONI), the Office of Strategic Services (OSS), and the Federal Bureau of Investigation (FBI)." The reports are a veritable he-said-they-said between the author and the FBI, mainly J. Edgar Hoover, who was its director for fifty years. Characterized as an inglorious perfectionist and virulent racist, he had a list of enemies of the United States 12,000 deep, including those of German descent, homosexuals, actors, musicians and anyone for whom he didn't care; for example, Walt Disney, Jackie Robinson, Howard Hughes, Charlie Chaplin, John Lennon, Dr. Martin Luther King Jr., Marilyn Monroe and Ernest Hemingway.

Papa's modicum of success with the anti-Nazi spy network he had set up in Cuba, inadvertently turned the spotlight away from

---

[169] Nicholas Reynolds, CIA Museum Historian, "A spy who made his own way," Ernest Hemingway Wartime Spy. *Studies in Intelligence* Vol. 56, No. 2

J. Edgar Hoover and the FBI's anti-mobster successes. He perceived Hemingway's actions as an "alarming intrusion into his FBI's territory," and his network as an attempt to control, mock and vilify him. For years, Hoover tried to discredit Hemingway, including asking the FBI to take "Any information...relating to the unreliability of Ernest Hemingway as an informant...discretely to the attention of Ambassador Braden. In this respect it will be recalled that recently Hemingway gave information concerning the refueling of submarines in the Caribbean which has proved unreliable."[170] See p.285) The FBI thwarted Papa's chances of succeeding with a proposed book on his experiences in espionage by portraying him as an "unreliable, pathetic drunk." However the bureau was not as efficient as they thought as they missed Hemingway's recruitment as a spy for the Soviet Union's KGB.[171] Notes, available online in Russian and English,[172] do make scant references to Hemingway or his code name, "Argo." Though contacted a couple of times, there is no evidence that he followed through or contributed anything to the Soviets. Perhaps because spies are discrete types with steely nerves and a natural ability to lay low and keep secrets, not impulsive, drinking men who talk too loudly and too much and look for fights.

Matters of the Heart

In addition to courting danger, Hemingway courted women for the special cocktail of norepinephrine, dopamine, phenylethylamine and oxcytocin that got him high. At twenty-two, he fell for Hadley Richardson, a shapely, feminine, outdoors-girl, a few years his senior from Saint Louis; he married her. On the wings of fresh love, they relocated to Paris for his *Toronto Star* assignment. The euphoric haze of their togetherness and the

---

[170] FBI files. Alexander Vassiliev, a Russian journalist, came across that tidbit in the Stalin-era records of Soviet intelligence operations against the United States in 2005

[171] Actually the less-known forerunner, thereof, the Narodnyy Komissariat Vnutrennikh Del (NKVD) (People's Commissariat of Internal Affairs)

[172] http://digitalarchive.wilsoncenter.org/collection/86/Vassiliev-Notebooks

move was enhanced by the birth of their son, "Jack." They settled into the constancy of marital bliss that, for Hemingway, wore thin in four short years. Hadley's adoration in which he once reveled became a damper on his high. "The better you treat a man and the more you show you love him, the quicker he gets tired of you,"[173] he claimed, but that was not exactly true. When they parted, he still loved her. He just didn't know how to love and be loved in a familiar union absent of the euphoria of newness. He hadn't invited an affair but when one came along, he didn't turn away. He embraced it and let it re-inoculate him; it was with Hadley's chic "friend" Pauline Pfeiffer. Pfife, as they called her, had vigorously hunted and caught him. A bit reluctantly, he joined the battalions who, for centuries, have crept up Paris' ancient backstairs to their lovers. To his regret, his betrayal cost him his wife. "I wished I had died before I ever loved anyone but her," he later wrote in *A Moveable Feast*, for he was genuinely tortured over his lust for his mistress and love for his wife. After Hadley had given him ample chance to sort out his feelings, which he was incapable of doing, she divorced him in January of 1927. In May, he and "Pfife" married, and she gave him two more sons, Patrick and Gregory, "Gig"[174] Collectively, she and the children traipsed in his sudsy wake to Spain and Africa, but his pattern repeated; the fix of Pfife faded. Their divorce was underway when he returned to his exciting indiscretions and re-met a brilliant, young journalist, Martha Gellhorn whom, few weeks after his divorce from Pfife, he made wife number three. Their common interests, lively debates and journalistic rivalry kept him high, but she would never be content to follow him and become a footnote in his life; she preferred to follow leads for herself which she did, and often. Almost immediately upon meeting Mary Welsh, who was married at the time, he proposed, and before the ink on their respective divorce decrees was dry, they married. As expected, a few years later their union was headed toward the doldrums. To steer clear, he unpacked his wanderlust and took her to Italy. The trip itself

---

[173] Hemingway, Ernest, *To Have and to Have Not*

[174] Gig struggled with transgender dysphoria, and later in life, underwent a sex change operation. He was then known as Gloria or Vanessa.

was enough to elevate his spirits, but then he met pretty, nineteen-year-old, Adriana Ivancich, and they were launched into full-blown orbit. While Adriana was but flattered by the famous author's attentions, he had high flown thoughts of more, much more. The prospect of a pricey fourth divorce stemmed his flight of fancy, and he limited himself to musing of what could have been with the charming, young, aristocratic brunette.

Adriana Ivancich, selfie, 1955

Bereavement

Hemingway was never alone in his life, Barring a little more than half a year, he had always had wife, or, fortunately, his animals. The big barrel chest of the man who claimed to kill animals, so he would not kill himself, housed a sentimental soul who, perhaps to his great benefit, kept a clowder of cats and several dogs nearby. Stroking them has been proven to have a positive, biological effect on human hormones decreases the primary stress hormone cortisol and increases oxcytocin, "the cuddle" hormone that lowers one's heart rate and results in a sense of comfort and calm. Papa's hillside estate in Cuba was covered with a cats, Persian, black, white, grey and tiger-striped and feral. He welcomed all who came and was grateful for their company as he wrote to Hadley, because "it is lonesome as a bastard when I am here alone."

Dogs were also lovingly afoot wherever he went: Paris, Austria, Kenya, Sun Valley or Cuba. He immortalized two, Kibo and Chickie who he penned into, *Garden of Eden* and *Islands in a Stream* respectively. While he grappled with the great metaphorical black dog, depression, he also had actual black dogs, Negrita, her puppy Lem and, his favorite, Black Dog. He was a Springer spaniel on the brink of starvation when he skittishly approached Hemingway at his Sun Valley cabin. He told his friend, A.E. Hotchner that despite the dog's poor condition, he "demonstrated

such polite canine manners and devotion, he was unable to leave him." In Cuba, he nurtured Black Dog back to health, and he became his loyal and constant companion when he hunted, swam, read or wrote. In fact, he claimed Black dog "was an accomplished author himself."[175] Though he grew old, he continued in his important role as protector of Finca Vigía. Sadly, his beloved best friend, Black Dog became a victim of international politics. Batista's anti-American soldiers killed him with the brutal blow of a rifle butt, and in so doing, broke Hemingway's heart into smithereens. His murder signaled to Hemingway that Cuba had ended for him. Moving from the city he had come to know as home, meant leaving all that he loved, his animals, friends, manuscripts, his boat...everything. Reluctantly, he made the harrowing decision and headed to Ketchum Idaho with the knowledge that he would never return. The stress of moving and losing Black Dog, in

Hemingway hunting with Black Dog/ Robert Capa

such a savage manner triggered a depression that must have seemed bottomless.

As he had previously in the face of grief, he attempted to distract himself with his writing, in this case, *A Moveable Feast*. In addition, he purchased two tickets for the Festival of San Fermín in Pamplona.[176] When he went to the doctor for a check up, he

---

[175] Hotchner, A. E, *Papa Hemingway: A Personal Memoir*, New York: Da Capo Press, p.17.
[176] After his death, the two tickets were found in his desk drawer.

was found to be in reasonably sound physical health for his age, just a touch of hypertension and mild depression. On the grounds of treating the hypertension, he was admitted to the Mayo Clinic in Minnesota, but that was not done. Instead, he was subjected to a torturous 15 sessions of ECT and released in utter ruins. Watching him, in this condition, clean his shotgun in the kitchen alarmed his wife, Mary. In addition, she and his friends reported he had become paranoid, that he suspected his car was bugged and FBI agents were monitoring him. His friend A. E. Hotchner said, "The goddamnedest hell."[77] Papa's records uncovered at the Mayo Clinic in Rochester, Minnesota disturbingly "indicate that the combination of medications given to him did not help but "contributed to the depressive state for which he was treated."[78] As he was not showing signs of improvement, Mary wanted to readmit him. On bended knees, he begged her "not to send him back for more shock treatments."[79] Nevertheless, she signed the consent forms and he was subjected to more brutally barbaric ECT's., according to Hemingway scholar, Dr. James Nagel, an unprecedented "thirty-six sessions" in all that produce the supposed desired side effect of retrograde amnesia. "The reduction of intelligence is an important factor in the curative process... the fact is that some of the very best cures are in those individuals whom one reduces almost to amentia (feeble-mindedness)..."[80]

To cure the disease and kill the patient is an unfathomable action which is in direct conflict with the classic covenant of the Hippocratic Oath to keep patients "from harm and injustice." Doctors knew they were tampering with the rare brain of a gifted, world-renowned author who had received the Pulitzer Prize and the Nobel Prize for "for his mastery of the art of narrative, most recently demonstrated in *The Old Man and the Sea,* and for the influence that he has exerted on contemporary style." Heming-

177 Hotchner, A. E., Papa Hemingway, a Personal Memoir, p266.
178 Reynolds, Michael S. Hemingway scholar and biographer
179 Dr. James Nagel, Hemingway biographer.
180 Myerson, Abraham. "Further Experience with Electric-Shock Therapy in Mental Disease," The New England Journal of Medicine 227(11) (Sept. 1942): 403-407.

way's mind was a precious object and the essence of his identity. To deliberately force irreversible retrograde amnesia on him was to commit murder, plain and simple. What reputable doctor could carry out such a crime? The answer came out when, in the 1980's, the FBI declassified its files[181] in accordance with the Freedom of Information Act; it was his own psychiatrist, Dr. Howard Rome.[182] FBI director J. Edgar Hoover long had his henchmen shadowing and monitoring the author's every move. Thus, though Hemingway entered the Mayo Clinic under an assumed name to protect his privacy, the FBI knew he was there[183] because Dr. Rome was their inside informant. Ernest Hemingway was not paranoid. His gut told him he had been under surveillance; he was for 20 years.[184]

Yes, he was depressed. He was coping with the profound grief for his beloved companion, Black Dog who had been so viciously murdered, and the transition from his home in Cuba to the States. As he writes in *Death in the Afternoon*, "The great thing is to last and get your work done." True to his words, he distracted himself from his woes and with considerable enthusiasm, to continue on *A Moveable Feast*. In addition, he had purchased two tickets for a return trip to the Festival of San Fermín in Pamplona,[185] a vacation spot he genuinely cherished which would have been the best way to cheer himself up. Psychiatry tells us that a person who believes committing suicide is cowardly, who is enthusiastically immersed in work and anticipating a future trip is not one on the brink of suicide. Perhaps the unnecessarily high number of brain-obliterating ECT's had, as it was supposed to, zapped away his vitality, his memory and his intelligence and rendered him irreversibly "feeble minded." His identity was inextricably intertwined with writing. To be face a life without it was to face death every day. The tickets he had bought months earlier to that year's festivities in Spain would go unused. Allegedly, Hemingway, who had *never*

---

[181] FBI File page 283
[182] Meyers, J., *Hemingway: A Biography*, 1985, London, Macmillan. p. 541.
[183] See Reference
[184] FBI files page 282
[185] After his death, the tickets were found in his desk drawer.

before mentioned or attempted suicide, took the shotgun with which he had so often hunted, and in a last act of control over his life or to express hostility against the tyranny that had been so callously and mercilessly inflicted upon him, blew away the skull that actually no longer held his brilliant brain.[186] This time, his soul had come out of his "body, like you'd pull a silk handkerchief out of a pocket by one corner. It flew all around," but it could not return.

---

[186] As with van Gogh and Marilyn Monroe, the jury is still out on the cause of death.

🌼 *Conclusion*

> "A tendency to melancholy..., let it be observed,
> is a misfortune, not a fault." [187]
>
> Abraham Lincoln

Prior to 1975 when I began researching depression, I had been under the assumption the cause was, in part, leisure time, that eons ago, hunters and gatherers were heavily engaged in locating food sources; knights jousted for ladies' hands; crusaders pillaged for monarch and church; explorers crossed oceans for unclaimed lands and on and on. Time for introspection and depression had to have been on the back burner, right? Wrong. Archaeological and anthropological researchers have found evidence of depression dating back to the second millennium. It reveals the exact same symptoms, inexorable sadness, anxiety, excessive sleep, bouts of crying, hopelessness and/or thoughts of suicide, for extended periods of time. (I don't know why I thought they would be different.) "The Egyptian Ebers Medical Papyrus" of 1550 BC theorizes a troubled heart to cause depression. When a "heart is afflicted and has tasted sadness, behold his Heart is closed in and darkness is in his body." While in Greece, an imbalance in bodily fluids[188] is blamed. Alleged cures were quite caring; hydrotherapy, a good diet, music, perhaps a little donkeys' milk, opium poppy seeds and even talking to someone. During the Middle Ages, blame shifted to Black Death, smallpox and leprosy and then with the advent of Christianity one more was added, the sin of demonic possession considered contagious. By then, attitudes toward treatment had traveled 180 degrees away from the ancients' coddling to cruel beatings, exorcisms and starving. If those failed, the

---

[187] Lincoln- letter to Mary Speed, his friend Joshua's half sister. 09/27/ 1841.
[188] The four humors of Hippocratic medicine are black bile from which the word melancholy is derived; yellow bile, phlegm and blood.

demonic spirit was killed by drowning or burning which, to the disappointment of many, caused the patient to be collateral damage. The view that the mentally ill were possessed by demons spilled over into the Renaissance, a four-hundred year period of conflicting perceptions and cures. Along side the witch-hunts and execution of the mentally ill, there was a revival of treatment through dietary measures.

While that idea was first introduced in ancient times, science has proven it still rings true. Brain chemistry is strongly connected to the digestive system. In the softball-sized stomach— yes, that small— 95% of the "feel good" neurotransmitter serotonin is manufactured. 95%! That process, studies prove, can be blocked by carbohydrate, sugar, artificial sweeteners, salt and transfats, and of course alcohol. In excess, all by itself, liquor causes neurophysiological and metabolic changes that can induce depression. Twenty-five percent of United States suicide victims are intoxicated, and a full 90% suffer with MDD at the time of death.[189] At the beginning of the 20th century, scientists turned to the brain itself as the source of depression. When their primitive practical application of theories proposing adjustments to the grey matter via "ice picks" or electrical current failed, they forged ahead and found adjusting the brain's elegant chemistry can diminish depression. It is so fragile that it can be damaged by traumatic experiences or by simply witnessing psychological, physical or sexual abuse. Hundreds of years later, causes and treatments for major depressive disorder remain more riddles, wrapped in a mystery, inside a golf ball

That is largely due to there being no "one" depression, one borne of genes is different from one that is reactive which is different from one resulting from TBI or induced by stress, abuse, neglect, drugs or alcohol. Further complicating matters, as revealed in the foregoing artists' mini psychological sketches, is that one depression can bleed into another, making it impossible to sort out. Marilyn Monroe's strong genetic leanings toward de-

---

[189] Conwell Y, Brent D. Suicide and aging I: patterns of psychiatric diagnosis. *International Psychogeriatrics*, 1995; 7(2): 149-64.

pression were compounded by the abandonment, abuse and molestation she suffered in her formative years. This made her vulnerable to loneliness and the stress of her high profile life as an actress and movie star. To cope, she downed a pharmacopeia of prescription medication and drank. While these may have temporarily anesthetized her anguish, they exacerbated her depression and interfered with her therapy, which was extensive. Vincent van Gogh's genes and dysfunctional home laid the basis for his depression which was bolstered by his being bullied by classmates and shunned by his family. By waterboarding his pain with vats of absinthe, he worsened his condition. Hemingway was genetically predisposed to depression as well as illnesses known to cause it, hemochromatosis, and diabetes. Multiple serious head traumas and an all-consuming, life long love of drink sank him into a complicated sea of MDD. Still, he knew how to put it aside by focusing on something else. And then, there is Abraham Lincoln who was, as the story goes, born to melancholy onto which abuse, neglect, shame, head trauma and grief in spades were heaped before he had the stress of the Civil War. What could have helped him? He had come to terms with sadness as part of who he was. He and Ernest Hemingway were successful in their respective areas of expertise, despite their conditions.

As of yet, there is no way to stop the transmission of genes that might do harm or prevent trans/inter generational trauma. Creating an ideal environment for each and every child to prevent neglect would be a wonderful dream, but it is impossible. Barring sports, TBI's are inevitable. However help is not beyond reach, for those with MDD. They can and must be proactive, be self-aware, eat more healthfully, drink less alcohol, if at all and take advantage of the talk therapy and medication that have evolved over the last fifty years. As seen in the foregoing chapters, finding what works best is a challenging journey that may include books, groups, therapy or medication and action on the part of the sufferer.

If only society would accept Lincoln's perspective that "A tendency to melancholy…, let it be observed, is a misfortune, not a fault," the sad-bashing might stop, the stigma lifted and the depressed could more freely seek and receive help. Steps toward creating that society less critical of those with mental disorders include better ways to communicate to and about depression and its sufferers. Likewise, depressives have to find ways be as proactive as they can to make their condition known to the right people and to alleviate the symptoms.

PART II
Talking
What to Say. What to do.

—Elodie, si je me noyais me, regretterais-tu?"

✗—Combien qu'y te reste d'argent?

(—Would you care if I drown myself?
— "How much money do you have left?")

🌼 Talking: *What to Say?*
Use your Phatic Expressions

"If the choices are to be sad or to be dead, I'll take sad every time."
"Get up and try to turn your own light on."

Winchinchala

Shortly after babies appear on planet earth, scripts are provided to help them become properly socialized beings. First, at home, they are introduced are the all-important social function words: please/thank you/hello/bye-bye/sorry etc. Children will them use their entire lives, hopefully. Next, usually in school, they acquire further vocabulary to play, get along with friends, function in class and participate in interviews for university. Later they may go to a mentor others they know for the language required to ask someone on a date, to dance, offer congratulations at weddings and graduations or condolences at a funeral and... There is no end to the need for les bons mots. "What should I say?" People want to know the script to be comfortable, to fit in, to look smart, to do the right thing and to get help. Once upon a time, there were taboo topics that had no socially accepted scripts such as pregnancy, miscarriage, abortion, rape, abuse and sex or sexual orientation, even body parts. Theses topics were only discussed behind closed doors. Now, fifty years after the 60's cultural revolution anything goes; for example, the size of Beyonce, Jennifer Lopez and Kim Kardashian's asses. And while most of us from the 50's, never said the word "vagina," maybe not even in the gyno's office, it is now freely bandied about, used in jokes, printed online, in texts and in, at least one instance, on a playbill, "The Vagina Monologues." But the topic of depression? That remains unscripted. As a result, no one knows how to bring the topic up, say they are depressed, and few know how to respond if someone says, "I am depressed."

Responders say anything, often doing more harm than good. For example, "No you're not. You're just having a bad day," denies the depressive's reality. Or they give empty advice. "Know what I do when I get depressed? I drink some herbal tea. That always helps me." Blame the depressive. "We all make choices. You have chosen to be miserable." Not helpful. If the person is truly depressed, they have probably been that way for days or weeks, so telling them to "look on the bright side," or "tomorrow is another day," are meaningless, and in some cases, frightening to depressives. "Oh crap. Tomorrow is another day?" Many days have come and gone for them, possibly excruciatingly slowly.[190] Thus they have the impression that they have been, and will be, in the dark forever and all eternity. Inexplicable changes in their personality and behavior are difficult to accept. "I'm not myself," they often say. As a result they become melancholy and anti-social; they shut down. That is to be expected. Depression is accompanied by a sense of worthlessness, extreme fatigue, the inability to concentrate, sleep or stay awake (insomnia or hypersomnia), find enjoyment in anything, (anhedonia) and or giving recurring thoughts of suicide. Anything can be a monumental task, the routine of getting out of bed, making a cup of coffee, answering the phone.... Depression is painful! (If you have not experienced clinical depression, these are difficult to fathom, but they are real.) Depressives (D) are not familiar with these feelings themselves and, as is the case with the unknown, they are scary. They do not want to face them, and they hope the condition will go away, like a bad experience or a nightmare. If they have been diagnosed with depression and acknowledge it, they worry about what will happen to them and anticipate dismissal, disbelief or negativity in

---

[190] Time alteration for depressives has been considered by psychiatrists since the 1920's However, in an experiment, Dr.'s Sven and Daniel Oberfeld have proven that time literally slows down. **Thönes, S.**, & Oberfeld, D. (2015). Time perception in depression: A meta-analysis. *Journal of Affective Disorders, 175,* 359-372,

the world, even among friends. Thus the condition encourages them to isolate.

As a friend or family member (FF) of an adult, one can sympathize, be patient and encourage the depressive to get help. Remember, one can not force anyone to do anything. Invite them out, despite their dark mood. Let them know their presence is important. As mentioned in chapter 4, before speaking in the name of helping, ask yourself the following. Exactly what do I know about diagnosing and counseling a depressed person? Am I able to identify the cause as head trauma, a physical illness such as hypothyroidism or hypoglycemia, too much iron, too many hormones or not enough? Can I help uncover a deep childhood trauma? Can I prescribe medication that will see one though? Will I be able to select the proper therapy and commit the time it takes? No. No. No. No. No. No. Guess what? Even if the FF was a psychiatrist, ethics would make the answer no. The therapist-patient relationship, rooted in confidentiality and objectivity, would be endangered.

For Depressives

If you are depressed, remind yourself:

I

I HAVE PERMISSION TO BE DEPRESSED and
I HAVE PERMISSION TO SPEAK ABOUT IT to the right person.
THERE IS HELP.
DEPRESSION MAY BE EPISODIC AND PASS or it MAY LAST.
Either way,
I CAN NOT JUST WAIT FOR THE LIGHT TO APPEAR.
I MUST GET UP AND TRY TO FIND THE LIGHT SWITCH.

IT IS NOT EASY.

Your depression, family or personal history or whatever the causal experience may reveal itself to be, should be only be shared in support groups with others who have had similar experiences and with the professionals who get paid to hear and analyze them. It is unreasonable and, actually, a little selfish to assume FF can handle stories of endless dreary days of despair, suicidal thoughts, flashbacks or abuse, not everyone can. That does not mean FF do not care. They do, but...

- Depression can be contagious, not just intergeneration-ally, but with anyone. Constantly being around D's and interacting with them alters those around them, can bring them down. (Perhaps that is why there is a high suicide rate among psychologists and mental health workers.)

- Such feelings may trigger unsettling concern or her own unresolved problems and make them uncomfortable.

- Listening may put them in an awkward situation because they may know the one or two people mentioned.

- Watching helplessly as a loved struggle through mental health problems can be painful, and it can impart secon-dary trauma on them.

- Most people do not know how to process their own psy-chological flotsam, jetsam and spindrift. They can not be expected to handle those of another.

What to say to colleagues (C) about your depression.

A person's mental health issues are inappropriate for the work-place. If you look very sad, a concerned colleague may comment. This is not the time to overshare. That usually overwhelms and repels others.

     C: You seem a little sad lately, Everything all right?

✓   D: Yeah. I am just going through something. I'll be fine.

Or D: Thank you for asking. I just have a lot on my mind.

Should your depression have already been made public, brush it off. The details are no one's business. Just reply:

✓ D: Thanks. I'm handling it.
     Or
   D: I found someone to work with.

Finding the right therapist is challenging (chapter 6), but until the "right one" comes along, one can see an *available* therapist or a psychopharmachologist for medication. (Meds do take time to work. Give them time.) Also there are groups and exercise, even something as simple as walking can help. Numerous studies have verified even moderate walking alleviates, symptoms.

ISOLATION IS NOT AN OPTION,
GET OUT YOUR PHATIC EXPRESSIONS. [191]

Phatic expressions are small talk. Almost everyone we meet asks, "How are you?" We automatically say, "Fine."

#1.   CONVERSATION

When FF's call, because they do care, dig deep, mind your manners and...

✓ ANSWER the PHONE and say

    D: Hello.
    F: Hi. How are you?
    D: Hanging in there. How are you?
    F: Not bad.

    END

---

[191] Anthropologist Bronislaw Malinowski defined those, as polite small talk, mundane trivial conversation, including nods and grunts; it is language that maintains bonds of sociality among people.

FF will want to see you. Do not worry about mood, personal appearance or how messy the house. If they want to see you, tell them okay.

✓ ANSWER the DOOR; let them in or say

D: Hi. How are you?

FF: Great. You?

D: Yeah. Good. I don't feel like visiting right now.

FF: Okay. As I said on the phone, I just wanted to know if you are okay.

D: Thank you. Let's talk on the phone soon.

FF: Sure. You're okay, right?

D: I am. You take care.

FF: I will. If you need anything, let me know.

END

#2.   **CONVERSATION**: Being supportive.

FF: How are you?
D: I don't know I didn't shake it, not yet.
FF: I am sorry to hear that. Have you been to the doctor?
D: I made an appointment. Have to wait a month.
FF: There are peer groups, aren't there?
D: I'm looking for one that's right for me...
F: I heard it doesn't have to be exactly the same, just one where people talk about how they are getting through their days.
D: I am looking into it. Thank you. So how are you?
END

3.   **CONVERSATION**: Suggesting therapy

D: I am not myself lately. Sorry I' am bringing you down.
F: You're not. No apology. You don't have to be any particular way for me to see you. That's why we're friends, right? Have you considered therapy?
D: Therapy won't help?
F: How do you know if you don't try it?
D: Discovering what depresses me could make me worse.
F: Therapy and meds have an 80% success rate.
D.   Meds? I won't be myself if I take meds.
F.   But . . . you are not yourself now.
D: Taking pills and talking to someone is not going to change anything.
F: Doing nothing isn't going to change anything either. Over-coming a problem is a journey.
D: Doctors, receptionists typists, everyone will find out.
F: That's why a lot of shrinks act as their own assistants. And the staff they hire use codes.
D: Still...
F: Okay. No pressure. Think about it.

END

✓ # 4.   **CONVERSATION:** Drop in visit: (Not recommended.)

D: So you just drop by?
F: We're concerned about you.
D: Don't be. I'm fine."
F: Then come out with us.
D: Why? I'll just bring everyone down.
F: So just sit there.
D: What for?
F: So you'll be with us.
D: What's the point?
F: We want you with us. The food is good.

Maybe the person will grab a coat and come. Or maybe he'll say:

D: I really don't feel up to it.
F: Okay. I'll give you a call tomorrow. Okay?
D: Around noon.
F: Okay.
END

✓ TIP: (Be sure to call. Continue to ask and to include them.)

✓ Going out with friends:

Bars and alcohol-driven parties are off limits. As with alcoholics and addicts, depressives must establish healthy connections. If one is invited to any thing else, a fair, a dinner, a movie, church...You should do whatever it takes to accept. If you do, the most important thing is to...

✓SHOW UP.

X *What Not to Say*

Be reminded, 18% of the population has experienced MDD. The other 82% have supposedly not. They are inclined to share what they have read or heard or seen a movie or what their great aunt Susan did to cure her depression which usually does not work. Best to keep such advice to yourself. Do not talk about what you do not know.

NEVER EVER NEVER ENCOURAGE SUICIDE.

X   You want to kill yourself? Go ahead. (Really bad idea. If those words come out of your mouth, apologize.)

NEVER SUGGEST ALCOHOL.

X "Let's go get a drink."

NEVER CRITICIZE

X   You look terrible.

This place is a mess.

We all make choices. You have chosen to be miserable.

NEVER BLAME THEM FOR THE DEPRESSION

Forget beginning sentences with "If you..."

X   If you ate better you wouldn't be depressed.

If you would be more positive, you would feel better.

If you had stayed where you were...

If you would leave him/her, you...

X NEVER TRIVIALIZE OR DENY THEIR FEELINGS

Oh, come on. It can't be all that bad.

Look at that man in the wheelchair. He's laughing. He can't even walk.

X NEVER USE CLICHÉS or INSPIRATIONAL QUOTES

When life gives you lemons, make lemonade.

It's always darkest before the dawn.

Tomorrow is another day.

After the rain comes the rainbow.

Such platitudes are annoying, not helpful. Ask yourself: Have I ever said one of these to anyone who has been depressed for a month and had them perk up and say, "Yeah, you know, you're right. I forgot all about that." Probably not. A depressed person knows tomorrow is another day, and they dread it because it will probably be as dark and painful as the last 43 or 355 or....

X NEVER THREATEN OR TRY TOUGH LOVE

If you don't stop this, you will never see me again.

Call me when you decide to feel better.

Knock it off! Act like yourself.

Snap out of it, will you?

A depressive is not thinking as clearly as usual. S/he can no more snap out of the pain and anguish they feel than cancer. Such comments validate their feelings of low self-esteem and force people into isolation.

X #1.   CONVERSATION: "Cocktail Party"

Several years ago, I attended a dress cocktail party. Loud voices from the second floor challenged the music, which the DJ, naturally turned up. Moments later there as the cacophonous crash of a door being broken followed by a terrifying scream. Within seconds, the news streamed down that a guest had tried to kill herself in the bathroom. The police and fire departments arrived. An officer gestured for the DJ to stop the music and barked, "Nobody leaves! Thanks."

  Rescue carried the young woman down on a stretcher. The white bandages on her wrists were soaked with blood.

HOSTESS: (To attempter on stretcher.) "Why did you do this at my party?"

MALE GUEST: (To hostess.) "Christ! What is wrong with you?"

HOSTESS: "Just another grab for attention if you ask..."

MALE GUEST: "What? We should have listened when she said, 'I really want to die.'
HOSTESS: "If she wants to die, that is not my problem. If you knew how many times she has put me through..."

MALE GUEST: "Put YOU through...?!"

HOSTESS: "Yes. Why doesn't she put us out of our misery and kill herself already?"

MALE GUEST: "With friends like you, maybe she should!?"

END

🌸 Personal Comment

Long ago, I saw a Charlie Brown comic strip that, though sad, made me laugh, I will never forget it. Charlie stands with his enormous head hanging over and his eyes staring blankly at the ground. His loudmouth friend Lucy approaches and asks, "What's wrong Charlie Brown?" Without raising his head, he tells her, "This is my depressed stance. When you're depressed, it makes a lot of difference how you stand. The worst thing you can do is straighten up and hold your head high because then you'll start to feel better. If you're going to get any joy out of being depressed, you're got to stand like this."[192] I laughed and laughed. Charlie Brown had validated my view that happiness is not guaranteed in life. We should not expect to find it. Others should not demand it of us. Some of us have to be "glad to be sad," as I often say. I got that from my father who never discouraged crying. If ever I apologized for tears over anything, he offered his sage words. "Crying is all right. You don't hold back laughter. Don't hold back tears." Each is an important part of the human experience, yet the world, especially the United States has long been embroiled in an annoying and dangerous assault on unhappiness. The claim is that one is responsible for one's happiness, that, "Happiness is a choice." Not really. Sufferers must be allowed to speak up, not to get happiness; that is not a guarantee, but to release their suffering. Talking to a trained therapist is one of the best methods. They can help one explore possible causes or suggest coping techniques which can improve the quality of one's life. Many are only in the throes of an episode of depression and may make a complete recovery; others learn to live with depression. Each person's journey is different. Like Charlie Brown, I have learned to find joy in my depression, accept that the negativity and gloom I feel at times is all right,[193] it is part of who I am. I mean, if the choices are to be sad or to be dead, I will take sad every time.

---

[192] Used with permission of Charles Schulz © PEANUTS Worldwide.
193 Depressive Realism Theory

PART III
Radiant Writing

Do it Yourself Soul Searching
Therapy/Preparation

"Oh! What to write? What to write?"

Radiant Writing
Do it Yourself Soul Searching/
Therapy/Preparation

A lifetime of learning, travel and curiosity has given me the opportunity to meet literally thousands of people. I enjoy talking and listening. To break the ice, I sometimes ask what they are reading or what fears they have. Not everyone is quick to answer the second, but when they do, it is quite entertaining. Seems, there is no end to what frightens people: clowns, the color yellow, marriage, vegetables, flowers, being alone, being rained on, crossing bridges, dolls...[194] Over time, I have found two of the most common are public speaking and writing, the former more than the latter. I suppose that is because it puts one in the position of being publically judged and criticized. As for writing, I hear, they never "know where to start," "couldn't spell," or very sadly, "...didn't have anything to say." People have more to say than they know if it's just for them, so that knocks out spelling. As for where to start, anywhere is a good place. Pick a day. Start with the weather, where you were, who you were with, anything. Just start.

Writing has long been considered an incredibly useful tool in psychology. As it turns out, the activity of transferring thoughts to a page, allows mental energy to stream through our arms and out our fingers. Empirical data supporting this comes from "Brain scans on volunteers [showing] that putting feelings down on paper reduces activity in ...the amygdala, which, as aforementioned, is responsible for controlling the intensity of our emotions...whether people elaborated on their feelings in a diary, penned lines of poetry, or even jotted down song lyrics to express their negative emotions."[195] Indeed, those who take the opportu-

---

[194] Names for these phobias in order are: Coulrophobia, xanthophobi, gamophobia, lachanophobia, anthrophobia, autophobia, ombrophobia, gephyrophobia, pediophobia. ..glossophobia and graphophobia.
[195] Keeping a diary makes you happier," guardian.com, Sunday, 02/15/09

nity to ruminate over their lives and jot down their findings can learn a great deal about how they arrived at being who they are.

Over time, therapeutic writing methods have evolved and proven effective. As early as the 1900's, Sigmund Freud viewed his patients' written replies as quarries of valuable information. In the 1960's, Dr. Ira Progoff designed an intensive journal method that popularized using writing and feedback as the central tool of therapy which is used in "Cognitive Behavioral Therapy" (CBT) that emerged about the same time. Over a designated period of twelve weeks, patients are assigned specific writing tasks. They then share those with a therapist/counselor who identifies where their negativity. Then attempts are made to retrain the patients' perceptions, so they can be more positive. For patients who trust easily, know exactly what is bothering them, want to write and share those thoughts, CBT can be helpful. For those who do not, James Pennebaker's "Expressive Writing Therapy" might be preferable. Clients write on themes chosen by the therapist for four consecutive days, devoting fifteen minutes to each session. There is no feedback. Personally, I am not sure what the benefit of that is, but it definitely allows one to vent.

I developed Radiant Writing which is free writing on a topic of your own choosing. I include suggested prompts in consideration of those who "don't know where to start." One need not follow them exactly. Of course, mechanics do not count. Many sufferers of MDD are not clear on what is bothering them. Yes, they are down and lethargic and in pain, but what brought that on? Genes, inter or transgenerational trauma, a death, what? The exercise helps writers explore what could be wrong by learning more about themselves. Also, it provide points to discuss with therapists and saves both time and money in sessions. You may start and find free-associating takes you completely off topic. No problem. Allow that to happen.

Prompts: (Only suggestions.)

Are there any to which you can relate? If not, make up your own. Then respond to the best of your memory. Try one. All you need are:

1.   The desire to try to write.
2.   15-30 minutes to start.

There is no writing limit on how long to write on a topic. However, if nothing spring to mind right away, allow the full 15 minutes before giving up. And don't be surprised if the answer comes to you hours later. As for length, there is no limit.

1.   Do you remember when your depression started? When?

2.   What people, if any, have you heard of or read about who survived horrific circumstances? How did they get through?

3.   Could there be trans/inter generational issues in your family? Why do you think that?

4.   What was the larger world around you like growing up? Did it affect you personally?

5.   Exploring childhood. Any strong memories?

6.   Do you drink? If so, when did you take your first drink?

7.   Letter to your children/grandchildren (Example on page 158.)

8.   Write a letter to your depression. Make a deal with it. Write a response. Answering this question for myself, I wrote "Depressionectomy."

9.   Where did your parents or grandparents meet? Would you consider their marriage an example of a good marriage?

10.   How would you describe each of your parents as people? If you were not their child, would you be friends?

11.   The circumstances of meeting a person important to you.

12.   What did you dream of doing when you were young?

13.   Describe a day in your life when you were happy.

14.   If you met you, would you have yourself as a friend?

If you are not ready to delve into your own life, warm up with a more external topic.

   Do you remember where you were for any of these events or one not here? What were you doing? How did you feel?

07/20/69, Moon Landing
09/05/72, Massacre at Olympics
02/11/90, Nelson Mandela freed
01/28/86, Challenger Disaster
11/09/89, Berlin Wall
12/31/2000, new millennium
09/11/2001, attack on the United States

15. Did you have any special feeling for a public figure or celebrity who passed? What did their life or death mean to you? (Suggestions below. Write on your own celebrity.)

John F. Kennedy,	Elvis Presley
Martin Luther King Jr.	Jim Morrison
Robert Kennedy	Kurt Cobain,
Marilyn Monroe	John Lennon

16.   What is the most memorable film you have seen? Why? Do you like the story in general? Is there something about the character that you associate with?

The Graduate 1967	Annie Hall 1977
Planet of the Apes 1968	E.T, the Extra-Terrestrial
The Godfather 1972	1982
Jaws 1976	Titanic, 1997
Star Wars, 1977	Other_____

The objective is to get in the habit of writing.

PART IV
Q& A Written responses
by
Winchinchala

What follows are examples, my answers to #1-5 Please note, for the purposes of this publication these were edited.

1. *When did my depression start?*

I don't know. For as long as I can remember, I have always been sad.

2. *What people have I heard of or read about that survived horrific circumstances? How did they get through?*

Prisoners of war. Just the idea is upsetting to me. Years ago, I read about the Bataan Death March, considered the worst atrocity of modern warfare. Yikes.

A. The Bataan Death March   B. The Trail of Tears

Soldiers carrying their dead comrades.

A. The Bataan Death March:

In the Pacific Theater during WWII, the invading Japanese Imperial Army had been battling fierce U.S. and Filipino troops. Many of the men were wounded or had malaria, but they didn't have enough water and food and were hardly getting any sleep. The promise that reinforcements and supplies were on their way kept them fighting. Unfortunately, Pearl Harbor had been bombed and the promise was impossible to keep. The supply ships couldn't reach them. Soon almost half the troops were no longer "combat effective"—defined as a man who could walk 100 yards without staggering and still have enough strength left to fire his weapon. Thus the U.S. General Edward P. King made the difficult decision to surrender on April 9, 1942 in effect saving the men because the Geneva convention which the Japanese had signed, stated captors were to provide POW's proper food, clothing and medical attention.

They didn't. Instead, they followed their country's ancient cultural belief that a soldier forfeits his rights as a human being if he surrenders. They buried their empathy and treated the POW's more inhumanely than a monster's imagination could venture. They marched the POW's, 76,000 ill and wounded Filipino and American men, twenty-five miles a day without food or water in 100-degree heat. "Those who fell were bayoneted. Some of those who fell were beheaded by Japanese officers who were practicing with their samurai swords from horseback."[196] Their comrades had to bear silent, helpless witness to these heinous acts, and in some instances participate. Survivors tell of having to bury friends alive who were too weak to get back up on their feet. In this way, 22,000 soldiers died on the way to the prisons. Once there, life was little better. But somehow, they hung on, not for a week or a summer but for more than three years! Of the 12,000 Americans held captive, 1,700 lived.

Note: The Human Mind and Spirit

I remain utterly amazed that even one POW lived. How? Did they have special genes? What had gotten them through that

---

[196] U.S. Congressional Rep. Rohrabacher, "Paying Homage to a Special Group of Veterans, Survivors of Bataan and Corregidor," Congressional Record - House, V. 147, Pt. 9, June 26, 2001, p. 11980-11985, at p. 11981

Hell?! Their narratives attribute their survival to luck, reminding yourself you had something to live for, hope, faith, comradery and a psalm and a prayer.

I love that, and at times when the black dog is visiting me, I turn my thoughts to these men and what they endured. If I wait, the universe will set me free.

B. Trail of Tears

The second feat of survival that came to mind is the Trail of Tears. President Andrew Jackson's Indian Removal Act was to free up Native land, so white Southerners could grow more cotton. To do that, he forced 46,000[197] Native Americans from their ancestral homes to an "Indian territory," now Oklahoma. A soldier, John G. Burnett, was stationed on the trail. When he turned 80, he wrote a "Birthday Letter" addressed to his children in which he recalls his experience. The following are excerpts:

***

"Being acquainted with many of the Indians and able to fluently speak their language, I was sent as interpreter into the Smoky Mountain Country in May, 1838, and witnessed the execution of the most brutal order in the History of American Warfare. I saw the helpless Cherokees arrested and dragged from their homes, and driven at the bayonet point into the stockades. And in the chill of a drizzling rain on an October morning I saw them loaded like cattle or sheep into six hundred and forty-five wagons and started toward the west.

One can never forget the sadness and solemnity of that morning. Chief John Ross led in prayer and when the bugle sounded and the wagons started rolling many of the children rose to their feet and waved their little hands good-by to their mountain homes, knowing they were leaving them forever. Many of these helpless people did not have blankets and many of them had been driven from home barefooted.

---

[197] http://www.pbs.org/He wgbh/aia/part4/4p2959.html

On the morning of November the 17th we encountered a terrific sleet and snow storm with freezing temperatures and from that day until we reached the end of the fateful journey on March the 26th, 1839, the sufferings of the Cherokees were awful. The trail of the exiles was a trail of death. They had to sleep in the wagons and on the ground without fire. And I have known as many as twenty-two of them to die in one night of pneumonia due to ill treatment, cold, and exposure. Among this number was the beautiful Christian wife of Chief John Ross. This noble hearted woman died a martyr to childhood, giving her only blanket for the protection of a sick child. She rode thinly clad through a blinding sleet and snowstorm, developed pneumonia and died in the still hours of a bleak winter night, with her head resting on Lieutenant Gregg's saddle blanket."

***

"They are kind and tender hearted and many of them are beautiful."

***

"The only trouble that I had with anybody on the entire journey to the west was a brutal teamster by the name of Ben McDonald, who was using his whip on an old feeble Cherokee to hasten him into the wagon. The sight of that old and nearly blind creature quivering under the lashes of a bull whip was too much for me. I attempted to stop McDonald and it ended in a personal encounter. He lashed me across the face, the wire tip on his whip cutting a bad gash in my cheek. The little hatchet that I had carried in my hunting days was in my belt and McDonald was carried unconscious from the scene."

***

"I can truthfully say that I did my best for them when they certainly did need a friend. Twenty-five years after the removal I still lived in their memory as "the soldier that was good to us". However, murder is murder whether committed by the villain skulking in the dark or by uniformed men stepping to the strains of martial music."

***

Murder is murder, and somebody must answer. Somebody must explain the streams of blood that flowed in the Indian country in the summer of 1838. Somebody must explain the 4000 silent graves that mark the trail of the Cherokees to their exile. I wish I could forget it all, but the picture of 645 wagons lumbering over the frozen ground with their cargo of suffering humanity still lingers in my memory."

"Let the historian of a future day tell the sad story with its sighs, its tears and dying groans. Let the great Judge of all the earth weigh our actions and reward us according to our work."[198]

December 11, 1890.

Note: Sharing and Writing.

The pain of the experience had stayed with him for over a half a century. Writing may have freed him of that. At the same time, he could lift any blame laid on him for following orders and participating in this cruel and wretched walk. As for the Cherokee: How did they get through? The answers seem to be support, faith, courage, hope and the strong belief that "It—will—end," or "This too shall pass."

"It—will—end," is another go to thought for a dark day. "It—will—end."

3. Any inter/transgenerational troubles? Why do you think that?

Maybe both, but I don't know that much about my grandparents on either side. Intergenerational was possible. From what I recall, our house was definitely tense at times. I don't mean from the usual parental spats, something else. I believe it had to do with my parents' youth and race. Laws regarding racial miscegenation, such as the Racial Integrity Act, can not stop love, but they can challenge young love and make life miserable. They got married in the 1940's, so they were only legally married in eleven

---

[198] Private John G. Burnett, Captain Abraham McClellan's Company, 2nd Regiment, 2nd Brigade, Mounted Infantry, Cherokee Indian Removal 1838-39

states; in the others, they were felons. That must have been difficult for them. many, neighborhoods, hospitals and schools in Massachusetts were unofficially "Whites Only." When mother gave birth to my brother, my father was not allowed in the hospital. Both related instances of the humiliating and demeaning treatment to which they were subjected for marrying out of their respective races. That would be hard for anyone, but especially for

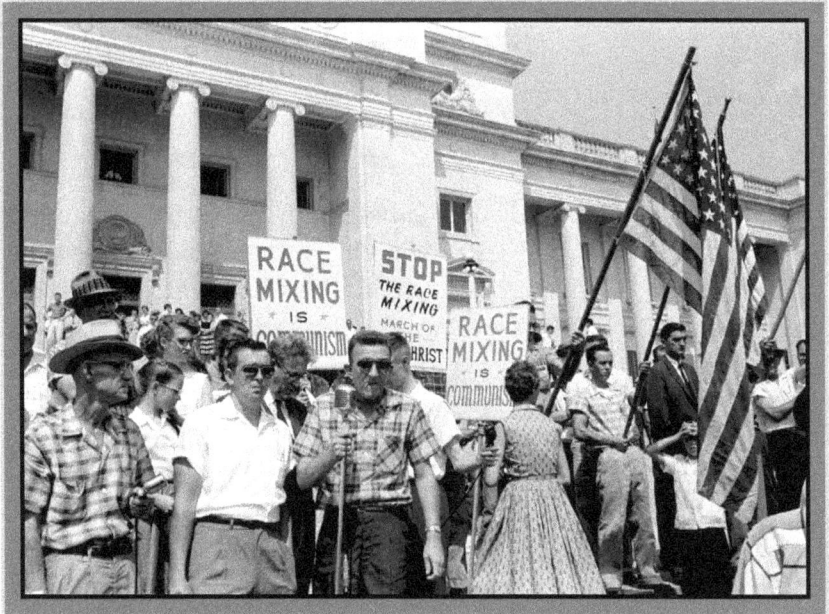

Protesting "Race-Mixing" at Congress

very young people. My father was around twenty and my mother, a teenager of eighteen when they tied the knot. Dad told me the police were free to stop them for walking together. When they did, they would separate them and ask him gruffly, "What are you doing with that white woman?" Of her they wanted to know, "Are you all right?" I did notice people gawk at our family and whisper behind their hands in the street and supermarket. Love has to be incredibly strong to bear up under such intense social pressures. Did they blame each other? Did they question their decision to marry? What about their parents? I know my paternal grandmother absolutely adored my mother, but I never met her mother or anyone else in her family. I was told that is because she did not marry a white man. That must have contributed to the tension. I was just a child. What did I know? I do know, eventually they separated, and that brought a completely different kind of stress. None of us knows what cards life will deal us. It is surprise after surprise.

4. What was the world around you like growing up? Did it affect you personally?

Though my mother was as "white" as one can be, I was often made fun of for not being white by students and teachers. The history books provided plenty of illustrations of half-naked savages for them to hold up. Because my father was indigenous, I was indigenous and that meant I was uncivilized, conquered or even extinct. They told me, "All the Indians are dead," so I was often called a "liar" for claiming to be one. Yet they also insisted on smacking me around for being one too. I really shut down, became a loner at a very young age. Those around me decided I was Mexican, Greek or Lebanese or Italian because I "looked like," one of them, and some of those groups took me in, Mexicans in particular. I never confirmed or denied what they thought, just let them think what they want. "If you can't beat' em, join 'em," right? "Go along to get along." Feeling alienated and unwanted is crummy for anyone, but those are memories I have from being five or seven or something. I wanted to fit in, to be invited to parties with everyone else. I was not. I will never forget the look on my mother's face the day a classmate's mother called to uninvite me from a party after she had heard from the other mothers that my father was not white.

I would say, the experience definitely affected my personality.

161

PART V
Narrative
(Answer to question 5)

by
Winchinchala

5. What was Childhood like?

I had an extremely complicated, fractured, non-linear childhood that took place in a wide variety of locations in the world. The more I wrote to answer the question, the more I remembered. I went back to it over and over again. Over time, I learned a lot about myself and the answer turned into a story.

To protect the innocent and not-so innocent, the names and dates have been changed.

Beat Sheep by Winchinchala 2011

Personal Narrative
The Beats & The Sheep

I didn't know anything other than my small world when I was a kid. Our apartment was a large, rambling place, but my room was cozy, prettily adorned with gauzy pink curtains and my own little library. There were beautiful trees that swayed outside the enormous windows, and I had French doors that led to a balcony. At some point Peter Pan started visiting, and he taught me to fly, with fairy dust of course. I always wished he would leave a handful, so I could fly to meet the American Indian Princess, Tiger Lily or wander in a distant forest. I always loved the woods. To practice flying, I would stand on top of the dresser wearing a sheet for wings and leap. I repeated the phrase, "I can fly," in several painfully unsuccessful, attempts. Perhaps a couple of those falls on my head, unreported to my mother, are responsible for memories missing from my earlier years.

My parents eventually separated. The split divided my existence between my mother and the conformists, the Sheep and my father and the non-conformists, the Beats. I had heard each group claim their way of life to be "the right way." The Beats were opposed to the sheep's "go along to get along" attitude that they felt perpetuated racism, bigotry, the acceptance of taxes, the draft, religion... They found their unquestioning behavior a threat to individuality. "They're all a bunch of sheep," I often heard them say. At ten, I was desperate to understand, so I might fit in. I tried to wrap my head around their disdain for sheep, especially because my mother was among them, but I was always left wondering.

What's so awful about sheep?

I wasn't even sure what they meant. *A sheep. Hmmm.* There were several pictured on the pages of nursery rhymes next to "Ba Ba Black Sheep" and "Mary had a Little Lamb." They were cuddly, tumbling creatures with the exception of the one in *The Little Prince*. Antoine de Saint-Exupéry's extraterrestrial royal requested a drawing of a sheep from the pilot he had met in the desert. He obliged with a few that the Little Prince rejected because he thought they looked "sick" or "old." When the pilot sketched an oblong box with air holes, which supposedly contained the animal, the Little Prince was satisfied. The Little Prince loved and missed his sheep, so I assumed they could not be all bad.

Once the Beats asked me if I knew what they meant when they referred to people as "sheep," I based my answer on that part of *The Little Prince*.

"Yes. They are easy to get a long with, live in boxes, and they don't ask why," I explained, and the Beats laughed. One of them acknowledged my answer.

"In a way, that's it exactly."

"So you hate them because they live in boxes?"

"First of all, no one hates them. We feel sorry for them. Their all oppressed. They've been brainwashed to believe the ways dictated by religion and the government is the way. It isn't. There are many ways, a person should be free to decide which way is right for him. Like me. I like this Buddhist idea. Follow a spiritual path to end suffering. Ya dig?"

I nodded though I didn't really "dig" all of what he said.

The Sheep on the other hand were quite harsh in their criticism of the Beats. Sexually immoral, subversives, deviants and drug addicts and sinners" are the words for them used by my mother's friends. "They're all communists," and "perverts up to no good," they concluded because, from what I could gather, they looked different. They wore dark glasses inside at night, which I thought a little weird especially because they liked to read so much.

I can remember their eyes through the lenses in candlelit rooms. My father's beat coterie was composed of the intellectual, creative, and literate of the day. Hardly anyone dropped by the house who was not covered in daubs of oil paint from her latest canvas, carrying notebooks of poetry, book of some sort or a camera. Though a child among them, they respected me, gave me a voice in their discussions, poetry readings, gallery openings. Everyone would chime in, and then someone would ask me, "What do you think?" They never judged or criticized me. I had to think for myself. I was part of the group. I even drank with them. I just sat my glass on the table, and they filled it. Every now and again, someone would nudge me to pass a joint that was being passed. Before long, I took a hit. For some reason, after a toke or two, the serious conversation to which I had been listening so intently became incredibly funny, not just to me but to others. I giggled and grinned and eventually woke up in the chair or on a mattress on the floor where some one had placed me.

These communal experiences of life, which began in Boston, gave me the sense that the whole city was a house. The coffee houses such as the Unicorn on Boylston Street, Club Passim or perhaps Club 47 in Cambridge, wherever we ended up, were like people's living rooms...with microphones. Though they were there and on, there was not always a schedule. Musicians came in from New York and played; poets read and drank coffee with philosophers and talked and talked and talked. After closing time, a group usually went to the home of whoever was closest. Eastern philosophy was popular at the time, and people didn't have much or feigned not having much to be cool and "with it." Not owning possessions lent itself to the carefree, nomadic lifestyle. Everyone always seemed to be "headed somewhere," usually where there were other artists, such as New York, Newport, California or Paris.

Such was the wandering, talented, cigarette/pot-smoking tribe that greeted me after grammar school; I was always happy to see them. With a Native American, Beatnik father and a Western European mother, my physical appearance was different from the predominantly white kids at school. No one knew what I was, so someone asked me on a daily basis. Tired of asking, I added a feather or two to my hair to announce my American Indianness. What was the harm in a couple of little feathers? None if a non-indigenous girl dressed up as an "American Indian" on Halloween, plenty if a girl wore one as part of her everyday clothes. As a member of the race the government had targeted for assimilation and annihilation, I presented a problem. I was told I could not wear feathers. How was I to know I had been born into a world of segregation and that forced indigenous people to hide and, at times, denounce their Indianness? My family had given me a white name to protect me?

My father made moccasins and beaded them himself. It took hours and hours. Everyone complimented him. I guess his father or grandfather taught him that, maybe his grandmother. Although when I think of my grandmother, I see her walking barefoot on the shore with her sisters, their long black hair in braids that hung over their shoulders. They walked along together for hours with pails and gathered quahogs. Sometimes, they pulled them out of their shells, rinsed them off and ate them right there on the beach. They spoke in their own language, which none wanted to teach me, again to protect me. Funny, I don't remember any thunder cracking in the sky when I was conceived to announce the union of my parents' alleged races[199] merging to make me, but I heard thunder on the day I was told, "No more feathers." It crashed through the sky of my universe and divided me into public and private identities. Suddenly I saw myself as an entity beyond the family in which I was a beloved daughter. In the larger society, I was a minority, demonized and consigned to a

---

[199] Race is a cultural construct. As a student of anthropology, I learned there is no biological basis for race. All humans are homo sapiens who share common descent. Differences in appearance are born of hereditary, natural and social environments.

life of discrimination because my parents had fallen in love; no one took my white mother into consideration when it came to my identity. Having been educated, I understand this was the result of historical events and attitudes that began with the colonization of the land most Native Americans call "Turtle Island."[200] At the time, it really hurt me. I felt particularly bad for my mother; it was as if I was not her child. I was sure to always tell her I loved her, though she was a sheep, a conformist. But my dad was a Beat. How could I be both? Maybe a wolf in sheep's clothing.

I am from the wolf clan, so it isn't too bad, but if I try to be a sheep when I am a wolf, I am living a lie. People will find out who I am and think I tricked them. It struck me that *If I am pretending, others are too. How do I know who is real?*

My questions went unasked. I did as I was told, and reduced my indigenous identity to make room for the sheep's costume. I eliminated words that my grandmother had told me from our native language such as tabatne, hownchaych, aunum, peeshkanash,[201] I no longer referred to The Great Spirit during mandatory prayer at school. When I was asked, "What are you?" I answered, "American." If any one insisted I was Italian or Armenian or Egyptian, I wrinkled my nose and ran off to play. I understood that to be a sheep I had to accept their misperceptions of me.

The Beats on the other hand never asked "what" I was. I preferred their company; though I noticed, they were sheep too because they conformed to non-conformity. They all had long hair, wore rumpled jeans and cotton shirts, sandals or boots, sunglasses and sometimes berets. In the end I answered how I already was both. I was a Beat Sheep.

---

[200] Use of the origin of this term dates back to the Legend of Sky Woman in Myths and Legends of the New York State Iroquois, 1906 by Harriet Maxwell Converse and Arthur Caswell Parker. However, the vision of a turtle as a country is found around the globe.

[201] Thank you, hello, dog, until next time.

Little by Little, the World
Sent me Away

In the fourth grade, in my mother's charge, my teacher called her to the school. Math problems had bested me; I ended up in tears that I held back everyday. Miss Grade School Teacher proposed I be in "Special Education," which tragically, at the time, carried an incredible stigma. My mother had never been to my school; she didn't really like to be bothered with such plebeian matters. Her petite stature, lady-like grace, light brown hair and captivating green eyes combined in just the right way to make her a beauty envied and targeted by less attractive and sophisticated women including Miss Grade School Teacher. Sizing my mother up, no doubt searching for faults, forced her face into an unflattering pinch. She invited my mother to sit, yet she remained standing, peered over her glasses and delivered her assessment.

"She is failing as you must have expected. As you know, children are retarded when one marries out of the race," she declared as if a tried and true fact.

To this minute, I can hear her emphasis on "the" when she said "the race." Her self-righteous attitude was backed the laws of the land.[202] The insult dropped my mother into a chair, and the teacher sat as well, so she could speak to my mother's face.

My mother's demure demeanor had deceived quite a few smug wisenheimers into thinking they could talk down to her and suffer no consequences. She had had enough. She arose so abruptly

---

[202] Interracial marriage was illegal and children of interracial couples were illegitimate in many states until 1967 when the Supreme Court declared the Constitution prohibits them from barring such marriage. In the 1960's physicist William Shockley and educational psychologist Arthur Jensen maintained genetic deficiencies in non-white rendered them less educable.

that she startled Miss Grade School Teacher. I was sure mother was going to slap her, but she didn't. Instead, she roughly grabbed my elbow, and we walked to the door.

"Now wait just a minute. I was talking," Miss Grade School Teacher called out indignantly. Her words bounced off my mother's back.

The teacher's chair legs barked on the industrial floor, and she hustled after us. I wasn't afraid. I knew my mother's power well. Once at a picnic, a dog had snatched the foil-wrapped chicken she had prepared. She didn't yell or say one word. She simply locked eyes with the animal. He dropped the container and backed away, exactly as the teacher did when my mother swing her head around and glared at her. Stunned the teacher took a step back and stood with her mouth open. Mother turned away and with me in tow, blew down the hall to the principal. She ignored the receptionist's protest and marched in with fury dancing off her small shoulders. The people with whom he had been speaking scrambled out. I was ordered to a seat near the receptionist, and Mr. Principal shut the door. He and my mother became frosted shadows on his office window pane. Every now and again, I could hear him say, "Yes, but Missus..." The receptionist slipped out. She must have blabbed something to the teachers because one by one they stuck their heads in for a quick listen to no avail. Mother and the principal's voices were too muffled. They continued through the first and second lunch bells. Later, I overheard mother tell a friend, "She has A's in English, Reading and Writing; she does not belong in "special education. The teacher is the one who is retarded."

I remained in regular classes and continued to excel in everything, well, except math. No one knew why I couldn't get it. Despite my mother vigorously denouncing the teacher's racist remarks and negative opinion of me, they lingered on, virus-like in my blood. Years later, I was diagnosed with dyscalculia, but until then, *I'm not smart and I cannot be smart because I am mixed*, was a thought which undermined my confidence and, at times, completely thwarted me from even trying. Students made fun of me, pulled my hair, tripped me, whooped like Indians, called me "half-breed," "mutt" and "Tonto." The teacher was not above displaying her amusement at their comments. The names didn't hurt as much as being invited to parties and then disinvited, for the simple reason a parent learned I was the girl whose father was not white. There were a couple of African American children who were always excluded but no other Native American children that I knew of.

Very often their parents, as was the case with mine, discouraged self-identifying in the name of protecting them from the painful slings and arrows and sometimes fists of bullies. I didn't realize the depth of some people's hatred until the first time the words "prairie nigger" were fired at me. Pow! Being shunned for no reason other than having been born to two people who loved each other is impossible for a child to internalize. To feel included, I sometimes hung with the African Americans or Chicanos or Moroccans depending on where I was. I accepted the identity of a Mexican, Italian, Greek, and Portuguese, whatever others labeled me. I didn't want to argue. African American kids viewed me as white, and while they didn't denounce me, they didn't embrace me either. They always pointed out, "You could pass," and to them, that was a barrier to friendship. In Europe I was totally stunned because they all thought "American Indians are great," and they wanted to play cowboys and Indians and themselves be the Indians. Mexicans never asked; they assumed because I looked like them, I was one. They were disappointed I didn't speak Spanish but accepted me. However, being accepted because I was thought to be something I was not made me uncomfortable. The seeds of disaffection had been planted in my soul. Rather than deal with the inevitable battle for acceptance by anyone, I learned to be a loner. After school, I found my own private places. In Boston, it was the public library or one of the Hayes-Bickford's, "The Bick" or "Coffee Corner" as we called it.

I invariably ran into one of the Beats there. If I wanted to be by myself, I had my own quiet spot in the library. There I felt I was surrounded by friends, the authors. Although sometimes, I wished I could ask them about what they had written. The same was true of musicians. One of the Beats had given me a really cool transistor radio for my birthday. It was small enough to fit in my pocket, so I could hear music when I wanted. One afternoon, I was people watching, and a song came on the radio. The singer's kind, sensitive voice captured my full attention. Its tenderness

suggested he needed the comfort his song provided. In a moment of illogical paranoia, I reached in my school bag to check for my notebook because I was certain I had lost it, and he had somehow obtained it. It really was if he was singing my words, but my notebook was there. Not only did he know all about the sense of alienation and hurt I was going through but also he had accurately come to the same conclusion I had. It was incredible.

I wondered what had happened to cause him to sequester himself away and not even cry. Suddenly I was happy about being sad because there were others like me. They had written songs about it and they were singing them, they were being broadcast on the radio. With an exuberant burst of excited prattle, I went to the Beats to tell them about the singer, Paul Simon and his lyrics. "Did you know that you could write something, not a story, but something really personal about yourself and describe how another person feels?"

Little by Little, the World Sent me Away

I have my books and my poetry to protect me
I am shielded in my armor
Hiding in my room,

safe within my womb,
I touch no one and no one touches me.

I am a rock, I am an island
And a rock feels no pain,

and an island never cries."[203]

They knew, but they were pleased I figured that out and said, "Writers hope for such connections, but don't expect them." The connectedness of human beings amazed me. To learn more about them I found I spent less time at school where I was unwanted and more time with the thespians, artists, musicians and Beats. Though from all walks of life, all ages, Blacks, Whites, Lesbians, Gays and foreigners, Japanese, Greeks and Frenchmen, they were all wrapped around the common spool of artistic expression. The musicians wrote incredibly thoughtful lyrics often half recited and half sung. They were filled with messages of equality, love and, of course peace. Those who were anti-war activists, whether communists or not, questioned the establishment which they considered elitist, pernicious and exclusionary, and they were proactive about changing it. Writers were the base of "the movement." Allen Ginsberg and William S. Burroughs inadvertently challenged censorship by writing without abandon what they wanted which is what an artist should write, including obscenities and descriptions of unconventional sex. Exercising their right to free speech landed them in court to defend it and take on the in censorship laws. The case was talked about in coffee houses

---

[203] Paul Simon Music in New York.

and our Beat group's intimate circle.

A Poet in Boston, 1951-1956 by Kimono Lukas[204]

On Fields of Force: Boston Commons   4: A.M.
Dropped, fallen
on the grass
like curling leaves,
inward drawn
against the dew,
the morning park
collects a group of
solitaries, bums
asleep in diagrams
drawn in lines across the grass.
From solitary point across to
solitary point, each
an inward drawn—up form,
each a forgotten, vulnerable world asleep
along the invisible lines of the diagram

Joan Baez & Bob Dylan, August 1963

---

[204] Permission: The Loukas Family of Massachusetts.

In my father's spacious living room there was a large potbelly stove around which the ever-growing coffee house cadre gathered after it had closed. Conversations sometimes lasted for days. In the morning, the tall candles from the previous night had melted into pools of wax in saucers or become textured streamers on Chianti bottles. Several became completely covered over time. Usually the flames had been snuffed out by the guests before they fell asleep in or out of their clothes in the living room. Years later, some of them had become celebrities, Joan Baez and Bob Dylan. From what I saw, they were young artists, little more grown up than I was.

The lot of Beats who I knew were altruistic citizens of the world bent on making it a better place. A great deal of breath and energy went into Civil Rights which included allowing Native Americans to gather, to practice their religion; the possibility of alien visitations; Eastern philosophy brought to us via Alan Watts and The I Ching book; the universe, abstract art, jazz, Gandhi, whether the U. S. should get more involved in Vietnam and on and on. The music and laughter of those days are heart-warming memories but those of poets reading are among my most precious. I was filled with a warm and wonderful sense of belonging. From behind the quasi-anonymity of those dark glasses, they brought forth their words with false bravado or read in voices quaking with insecurity; some edited on the spot and then continued reading. It was thrilling to be there as they were creating. No one spoke when a poet read. The only sounds were puffs on cigarettes, sips from glasses or the shuffle of shoes on the floor. If we liked a piece, we didn't clap but snapped our fingers to spur the poet on. I stood up one night to read a poem, and I hesitated for the longest time. I decided I should sit down, but the audiences loud collective snapping kept me at the mic, and I read.

A wood,	A leaf
A path,	A glance
A hand	A smile
A nother.	A nother.

Because I had physically blossomed by the time I was eleven, I had no trouble getting a job. I was at the Unicorn so often, George, the owner said, "You should work here." So I did. I made pretty good money; that meant freedom. But it was short-lived.

My mother had been calling to check on me, but no one ever answered. Then she called my school and learned I had been ditching She didn't blame me; she blamed my father and demanded I be returned, more as an act against him than anything

else. As it is with children of divorce, I was a pawn in a game between feuding parents. Returning to my mother meant returning
to school, and because I had missed so much, I would probably be
placed in the fourth grade instead of the fifth where I should have
been. Along with my independence, I would lose my drawing
classes at the Museum School. Leaving would be the end of the,
the Beat girl I had become, the "young one," "the jail bait," as
some men called me, dressed in black who wore dark glasses and
a feather in her hair.

"La Croix Rouge"

Separate Exits

"Not till we are lost, in other words, till we have lost the world, do we begin to find ourselves."

Henry David Thoreau[205]

I suppose as long as there are students, and they need to carry things to school, there will be lockers. And as long as there are lockers, there will be locker checks. That is how it was eons ago when I entered the ninth grade and how it still was a couple of decades ago when I briefly taught high school. The checks are part of administrators' duties for the stated purpose of monitoring students and the unstated purpose of finding contraband such as drugs, weapons or food. The process imbues school leaders with a false sense of control and brings a bit of excitement to their uninspired routines as it did Principal Toupin when I attended high school. Behind his back, the well-known, secret nickname for him among students was Toup, pronounced Toop, because he perched a hairpiece on his head. Perhaps when his hair began to fall out; the color, matched his own but it no longer did. Critical teens that we were, we concluded he was oblivious to its fake appearance or too cheap for an update. The mousey brown toupee sat atop his thinned, graying ring of hair like a small unkempt animal.

On the lapel of his suit, shiny from wear, he sported a miniscule "I Like Ike" button, though it had been years since Eisenhower's landslide victory over Stevenson. The button, bad toupee and tired, conservative suit marked him as a member of the establishment. Whenever our paths crossed, he eyed me suspiciously. As a long-haired girl in gobs of eye-makeup, black tights and miniskirts who carried books by Alan Watts and Jack Kerouac, he perceived me to be part of the counterculture, Beat-

---

[205]Thoreau, Henry David, "The Village," *Walden or Life in the Woods,* Tignor and Fields, Boston: 1854

niks and Commies. I was certain he secretly prayed for the day he would find a joint, a bud, or even crumbs of weed in my things, so he could expel me, or at least have a good reason to kick me off the student council. Unfortunately, for Toup and my opponent for student council president, Dana Gates, who wore a blazer to school every day and carried a bible, the counterculture was in vogue. Students were ready for something new, and that is what I offered when I ran for president. My platform of free speech and equal treatment for all students resonated with them from athletes to Chicanos to the handful of African Americans to the two Jewish kids.

Unbeknownst to me, my unconventional life had prepared me for the challenge. Dana got up and buckled under the mere pressure of the lights and the crowd. He stammered and stumbled through a speech he promised "will knock you out of the race." I wasn't afraid; I had spoken in public, in front of total strangers. At cafes and jazz clubs, I had witnessed authors reading their poetry and delivered my own. Lights? No problem. I wore my dark glasses. I also brought an accompanist, a trick I had learned from the Beats. There was no rule that we had to go on stage alone, so when a fellow student, Dennis, an aspiring bongo player, asked if he could join me, I agreed. We rehearsed which words in my speech he would emphasize. "We" was one of them. Safe behind my dark glasses with my friend nearby, I felt confident. I stood in front of the student body and they all applauded. I raised one of their complaints; "teachers' pets" being allowed to improve their grades with do-overs or extra credit work.

"We were all given the same work, and we all turned it in at the same time. We received a grade for that work done in that time." When I said, "we," I swept my arm out over the crowd and Dennis emphasized with a "Kak Kak Kak" beat on the drum. I continued. "The papers are returned with a grade. But "Kak Kak Kak" that is not the final grade for all of us. Certain teachers encourage their favorite students to redo and resubmit their work. That is why they are getting A's. And I don't mean one of the Pioneers who had to bring us to victory..." "Kak Kak Kak Kak Kak," Dennis played along with cheers for our football team, "or someone who was sick or had a real reason not to get the paper in one time. Of course they deserve a chance, but when a teacher only offers the opportunity to a niece or ..."

"Egg head Egbert," one of the beefy jocks bellowed as he jumped up and pointed to the pale, slim bespectacled boy in the seat behind him. "You little kiss ass!"

"That will be enough," a teacher cried out.

"Let him talk," I demanded.

"Think you're so smart. I've seen you carrying Miss Miller's crap to her car. You weasel."

As his teammates calmed him, I planted a noisy juicy smooch on the microphone. "Many teachers help their pets." I kissed the microphone again, and the auditorium busted up laughing. I wanted to continue, but my mic was cut and two teachers with Principal Toup rushed toward the stage. A few students jumped in front of them, linked arms and blocked their path. I went on without the mic. Dennis must have been high; he just sat there cool as could be. Figuring I was already going to be expelled gave me the courage to go out on a limb, way out. At the feet of the Beats, I had learned about the obscenity trial over Ginsberg's book *Howl* due to its references to illicit drugs and sexual practices that censors deemed egregiously vile. Though I had heard the Beats rail on for hours about the First Amendment and recite numerous lines from other banned texts, I was too embarrassed to have ever repeated Ginsberg's line anywhere until that day.

"Why are they trying to censor us? I mean a judge decided the author, Allen Ginsberg[206] can write balls, and bullshit..." sounds of shock and wild laughter filled the auditorium, "...and cock..." I stared right at Toup. "I'm just trying to get justice for my schoolmates. Can't I speak?'

In a seething frenzy, Toup sputtered.

"Young lady, do not mention that lewd, disgusting trash!"

I cupped my hands over my mouth and asked the audience, "Can I speak?"

---

[206] Ginsberg's poem Howl had been banned as obscene but On October 3, 1957, Judge Clayton W. Horn ruled that the poem was not obscene.

"Let her speak. Let her speak," They chanted, while Dennis accompanied their stomping feet and clapping hands with his. "Kak Kak Kak Kak Kak." "Let her speak. Let her speak"

In order to quiet them, one of the teachers signaled to have the microphone reinstated. Toup remained nearby to snag me when I finished. I knew I had to wrap it up fast.

"Thank you everybody. Remember, a vote for me is a vote for you because it is a vote for equality! Go Pioneers!"

Absolute hullaballoo ensued. Knowing full well we were hungry teens, and it was lunchtime. Toup stepped up to the mic, and simultaneously put the kibosh on the crowd's raucous, juvenile glee and punished them. He announced in his dry raspy voice that, "Lunch will be delayed today. First, there will be a locker check." The students switched from jubilating to boisterous grumbling and grousing. Though Toup spent an inordinate amount of time searching my locker in particular, he didn't find anything. That fall, in a close election, I became student council president.

✳ ✳ ✳

In the spring, Toup sprang another locker check on us before lunch. Each student opened his locker and faced the hall. He was so determined to find something, anything, that he called, the police and their drug specialists, two trained German Shepherds. They sniffed out Dennis' nickel bag of weed, and an officer escorted him out off in handcuffs. Everyone knew he and I were part of the same small clique, so Toup was sure I too had a stash, though the students all knew I didn't smoke at all because of my asthma. While I didn't have any drugs, I did have *Screaming Yellow Zonkers*. I loved the bright yellow kettle corn, a lot of us did. It came in a black box with wild designs and silly expressions that made us laugh. "Open the top, and turn the box upside down. If the *Zonkers* fall out, this is the bottom. If they fall up, this is the top. If nothing happens, this box is empty."

Humorous or not, we weren't supposed to have food in our lockers. I held my breath until the policeman announced, "Clear."

Skepticism stepped Toup forward. He unclasped his hands from behind his back and deftly stuck one in my locker. He pulled out my black box of *Screaming Yellow Zonkers.*

"Ah Ha! Contraband!" he announced.

"No. Those are *Screaming Yellow Zonkers*?" I corrected quietly.

Giggles ricocheted around the students watching.

"I don't see anything funny here," he declared gesturing at me with the box.

A few of the bright yellow pops fell out. I didn't want to stand there and be berated for a box of popcorn, so I snatched it and bolted down the hall toward the front door. Toup ordered the police to send the dogs after me. They refused on the grounds that trained dogs were to sniff out drugs, not chase after teenagers. Toup ran after me himself. Through the little squares in the cold, hard, industrial doors, I saw the warm, fresh, green lawn beckoning me. Then, I heard the collective thumping and thudding of the students following en masse. "Run for it!" one of them urged, and then the collective lot of them spurred me on, "Go! Run. You can do it." And I did. I was the wind. I blew down the length of the corridor and out the door, a gentle flurry of *Screaming Yellow Zonkers* in my wake but not Toup. He had fallen behind. Several students had made it to the upper reaches where they kept me informed on Toup's location while I caught my breath and decided which way to go.

"Take your time. He went to the office."

"Probably gonna call your mother."

"Don't say that. Have you ever met her mother?"

"Thanks guys," I said.

A gentle rain sprinkled down from the light grey sky. I sought refuge behind the hedges in front of the side door. Suddenly Toup burst out, and lashed at my arm. I dodged him to the delight of the kids in the window, but I could see I was trapped. I feared I could be arrested, though for what I wasn't sure. He leaned away from the rain and his toupee flipped straight up sending the students into a cacophonous uproar of amusement. It was clear that escape was only possible through the hedge. Just then, I heard Wes's muffler, Star, his dog barking excitedly. He had a black souped-up 1962 Plymouth Fury, and he liked to let everyone know it. At seventeen he was several years older than me, but my precociousness closed the gap, and we got a long very well. He reminded me of other teens among the Beats back east. I thought he would have been a better fit with them than the suburbanites out west. He had dropped out over a year ago, so I was shocked, but ever so glad, to see him at school. Fooling around, he gunned the engine and the car bounced on its chassis. Several of the guys hollered.

"Wes!"

"Hey man. How ya doing?"

"When ya coming back?"

From the driver's side, he waved and greeted Toup as only he dared, "Toupy! What's happenin' man?" He had sized up the situation and averted Toup's attention from me.

"You had better keep going Wesley," Toup warned, "the police are here....with their dogs."

"Me too," Wes told him and Star barked.

 I hesitated.

"Just do it," Wes urged in his strong, quiet voice.

Toup started toward me, but luck intervened. The bottom of his jacket was caught in the door. Someone would have to open it to free him. I raced for the Fury. Wes opened the car door. The students were wild with excitement. Toup was loose and racing after me. I jumped on the car seat, but before I could get completely in, Wes had slammed his foot on the accelerator. The car blasted off with such force that the front end lifted up a little and the door swung out with me on it. I held on tightly while Principal Toup stood on the sidewalk holding his hair down. And then he hit me the only way he could.

"You are off the student council—forever!" he shrieked.

He won. I couldn't do anything but focus on not falling off the door. Star barked and barked until Wes slowed down to allow me to get in properly. I did, and then he banged a sharp u-turn in the alley and arrived back on the street so quickly that time appeared to have stood still. The students and Toup were right where we left them in the windows and in the street. The muffler announcing our return elicited a glad roar from the students, and Star chimed in. Toup put one hand on his hips and held the other up like a traffic cop. Wes deliberately aimed the car at him and pressed his foot on the gas.

"No!" I screamed, "Jesus Wes! What are you doing?"

Wes' shaggy hair hung over his face, and he was sobbing. I shoved the steering wheel as hard as I could toward his door, and we went around on two wheels. I thought the car was going to roll over. Star yelped and slid across the back seat. We came to a stop and were stunned for a moment, and then Wes laid into the horn and backed up. Toup's arms spun windmill style as he dove for cover. Luckily the rain began to pour and drove him back inside the school. Wes maneuvered the car to the right direction on the street, and somehow, he laid a patch of rubber on the wet street.

After a time, he rubbed my leg and assured me, he "wouldn't have hit him."

A sentimental song, "Soldier Boy," about a girl professing her love to her guy, in the army streamed out of the radio. I sang along softly and every now and then, Wes and I exchanged a smile, but we didn't say anything, as was our way. We just enjoyed the damp spring breeze blowing by the windows. A downpour kept us in the car when we arrived at his house. I asked him what he was doing at the school since he had dropped out. Flicking at his corduroys, he confessed to having quit on an impulse and "I kinda regret it." He had driven by because he had nowhere else to go; everyone he knew was in school or had graduated and gone into the military or to college. His parents insisted he finish school; he didn't think he could "get back into that groove."

"My father told me, 'You stupid ass, you'll amount to nothin', but not here, not in this house. I won't have it.' What does that mean? I should go someplace else to amount to nothing?" Wes shook his head and sighed.

Another wave of grief overcame him, and in trying to hold back tears, his forehead knit together but he failed. He flicked them away and changed the subject to soldiers. His birthday was at the end of the month; at eighteen, he'd be eligible for the draft.

"Nam? Don't go. Roger Garcia came back in a wheelchair and Alan, Tom and Jimmy..."

"Came back in boxes. I know. I went to the funerals." He reached over and held my hand. "Hey I got a new LP."

Star let out a sharp bark. He was a mutt; his scraggly fur and mottled coloring suggested he was a cross between a beagle and a collie. Perking up his huge ears, he leaped out the car window and barked at Wes before going through his doggie door. Wes and I took the stairs to his living quarters, "the cave" in the basement. Star dragged himself friskily back and forth across a big towel on the floor to dry off. The black air glowed red from lamps Wes had covered with his mother's old scarves; they cast shadows of their printed flowers on the walls. He ran upstairs to see if anyone was home, and returned with a bottle of ginger ale.

"I guess mom's at the neighbors."

The LP had a folksy bluesy feel and a couple of the songs were about death, not exactly dance music, so when he extended his hand in an invitation to dance, I declined.

"Why not?" blasted out of him so loudly, I jumped.

He raised my chin and looked right in my eyes. "Sorry."

"I would, but I am not a good dancer," I confessed.

"So what? It's just you and me..."

When I joined him, I felt his strong, slim weight relax in my arms. The heat from his body melded with mine, and I tried to remember the last time anyone had demonstrated any affection toward me. None came to mind. I held him tightly.

"It's nice, isn't it; to hold someone, just to hold 'em?"

I nodded. The dark song seemed to deepen Wes' terrific melancholy, and it rubbed off on me. To conclude our dance, he spun me around, and then led me to the bed. We stretched out and exchange telepathic glances that said little other than we were comfortable with each other. He pointed out his favorite shadow.

"Isn't that far out?"

"What, the angel?"

"Exactly, but on the scarf, it's a flower."

"Yeah," I agreed and we fell into silence. Star snoozled between us. "So what do you think you'll do?"

"I don't know. Dad wants me out of here, and even if I did find a job..." he pulled a couple of official-looking papers from his pocket and dropped them on my arm.

I read, "Order to report for Armed Forces Physical Examination. You are hereby directed to present yourself... They already called you? Well, don't go!"

"Second page," he said flatly.

"You are hereby ordered for induction...What? Ordered? But you aren't even eighteen yet."

"I will be within thirty days."

"What did your father say?"

"I'm not telling him anything about my life."

"I know. You can go back east. My father's friends could help you get to Canada or..."

"No. No. If I go in, I could get my degree, a little money. I just don't wanna die in some jungle a million miles away."

"If I was a boy, I would go with you."

"Ha! If you were a boy, you wouldn't be lying here." He leaned over and placed his lips on mine sending a warm tingle through my body all the way to my toes.

Sounds from the kitchen above announced Sheila, his mother, had returned. They never talked, only argued, so we slipped out for a ride.

"Where's that a notebook of yours? read me one of your poems, will you?"

I fished it out of my bag and leafed to one I had been working on. "This is called face.

A mouth
opens & closes
reveals and conceals
the truth and lies
right below the eyes
that see when
opened or closed
but also don't when

opened and closed
on a face
door to the heart
door to the soul
door to the mind
always open
always closed."

He laughed. "Far out. I really like it." I beamed proudly, and he took my small hand in his. "I really like you."

"I really like you too."

He kissed me and draped his arm around my shoulder. For the rest of the afternoon, we sat listening to the radio and watching the rain on the windshield. When he dropped me off at home, we agreed to meet the next day to hang out in the park if it stopped raining or see a movie if it didn't. However, my mother had a third option, for unbeknownst to me, while I was lolling away the afternoon with Wes, Principal Toupin had called.

I slipped up to my room without seeing her that night, and she did not appear in the morning. In front of her seat at the breakfast table was a note reading "Suspended! Call when you get there." Along with it were an airline ticket and cash. Though I knew there was no excuse for my behavior, I wished I could have seen her, given her a hug and apologized before I left. I was sorry. My antics must have truly embarrassed her, my lovely lady sheep mother. She didn't have the patience and energy required to have me underfoot or to get me back into school. I wrote "Sorry," on the back of her note and left to meet Wes.

Our planned meeting wasn't until later, so I went directly to his house with a bouquet of flowers to add a touch of color and life to his dark basement, "cave." I would again try to convince him to go with me, to meet the Beats rather than ending up in the justifiably dreaded jungle ditch in Vietnam. With such an ear for music and poetry, he could learn from the Beats, feel the joy of being himself and belonging. As I rounded the corner, I saw two police cars on his street and several neighbors outside facing house. A middle-aged blonde in a robe sipped from a coffee cup, nervously descended her steps and approached me on the sidewalk.

"Flowers," she muttered to herself. "That reminds me, I have to pick up flowers," and then asked, "Do you know what's going on?" I shook my head A brunette woman, who I recognized as Wesley's next door neighbor, tip-toed slowly toward us and the blonde asked her, "What is going on?"

"Oh my God. What a shame. Poor Sheila."

"Why 'poor Sheila'? What happened?"

Beneath her voice the brunette said, "It was horrible." Though it was only 10:30 in the morning, she pulled a small silver flask from her pocket and splashed shots into their coffee cups.

"Oh my God. That bad?"

She nodded.

"Tell me!"

The brunette took a long swig from the flask. "Sheila called, absolutely frantic, so panicked I just dropped the phone and ran over." She took another swig. "I got there just as they were cutting him down from the rope..."

"What rope?"

"In the basement."

I felt light headed.

As if far far away, I heard the blonde ask, "The father or the son?"

I already knew, and I whispered it out loud, "The son..." as my heart dropped into my stomach, and I sank onto the steps. All of a sudden, I couldn't hear anything. A painting of Christ illuminated in my mind. *Why Wes?! Why?* I asked him. I hoped God would welcome my sweet friend, Wes and his dog into Heaven. *The all mighty Lord would not send a kid to Hell. He would know what a cool guy Wes was. He would want him there, wouldn't he?*

My hearing returned as the brunette said, "Yes, the dog too."

"So he hung the dog?! Oh my God no!"

"No. He didn't. Sheila told the police it had been hit by a car."

"Is that why the boy did it? Because of the dog?"

"I don't know. I really can't imagine..."

Anyone who was still home was in the street watching the medical team slide the gurney carrying Wes' sheet-covered body into the ambulance followed by a box which must have held Star. *Oh. At least they will be together.*

I have no memory of going home, packing, boarding the plane that afternoon or anything about the flight, only crying quietly by the window. A month later, my mother, who was still angry, called to tell me "A package arrived for you. I forwarded it. That was all. It was the LP with the folksy bluesy songs. A note that appeared to have been crumpled and uncrumpled and crumpled and uncrumpled again was stuck inside.

I Guess this is Hi and Bye I CAN HARDLY see iTs So DARK. AND THE Lights ARe oN too. thars How iT is All the Time. exCepT yesTerDAy. THAT WAs Cool Being with you, I Feel Like You get Me. You shouldn'T. I'M NoThing. ThaT's Me, NoThing iN the Dark. I WAS SoRRy TO MAKe You cry. Better You DoNiT KNoW Me, Better No oNe Does. You hiked the LP as Much as Me. iT's yourS. I Guess i love you AND STAR. ButT this is Hi and Bye.

Wesley

IF TheRe is something oN the other side. I'll let you KNow, ITs NoT your FAult. oKAy?

To this day, I wonder about the sequence of events. Had Star run into the street and been hit before Wes "died," or had Wes died and then Star ran into the street?

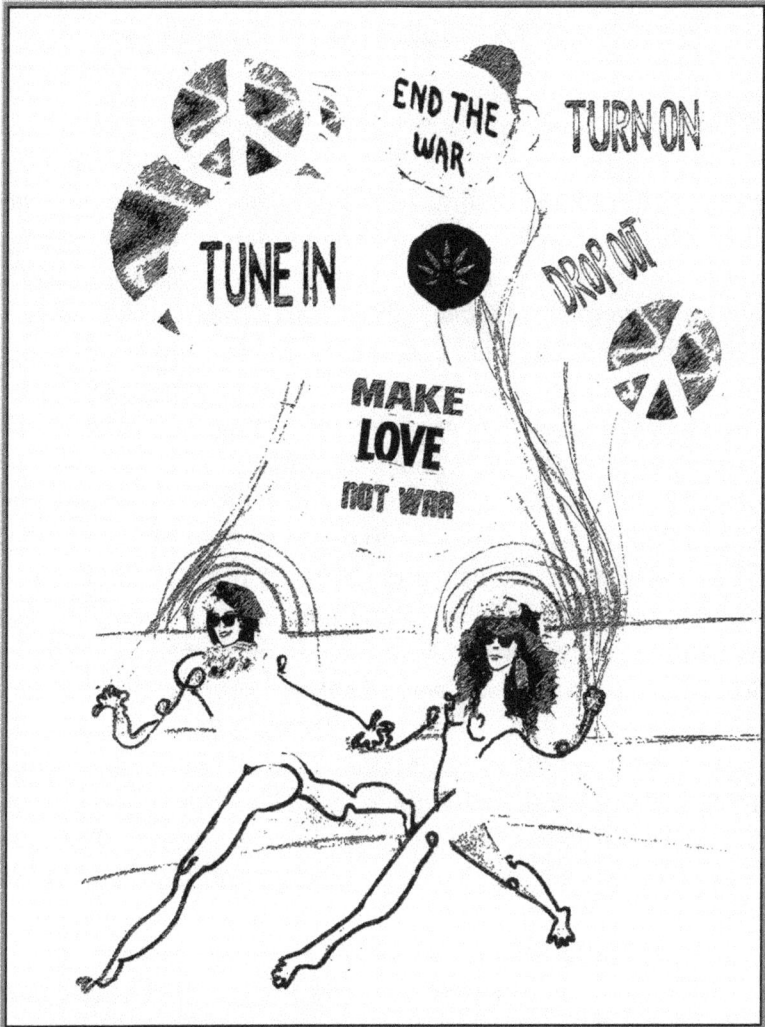

© Summer of Love, Artwork by Winchinchala
1965/2011

❀ "Summer of Love" a Moment in Time

The trajectory of my life ran through the Beats right into the Flower Children of the 60's, a time that also included organization intent on radically changing society's structure and values. The most well known are the Students for a Democratic Society, SDS; the National Organization of Women, NOW; Vietnam Veterans Against the War; the Gay Liberation Movement, Black Panthers and the American Indian Movement, AIM, even Hippies[207], who were not a formal organization, consciously demanded change by protesting. "Down with the Establishment," "Make Love, not war," Haight[208] [sic] is Love" and promoting "brotherhood," so that no one suffered; it was noble cause, and our world today is a testament to their success.

Among those consciously attempting to institute change were those who had unwittingly become part of the movement, those who had runaway from abusive or neglectful situations, castaways who had aged-out of foster care, displaced souls, without a home who wandered, "Like a complete unknown. Like a rolling stone," as Bob Dylan sings. They were taken in by the network of Hippie communes that stretched from one end of the country to the other and eventually spread to Canada and Western Europe; it provided an easy way to "Tune in, Turn on and Drop out," as the LSD guru, Dr. Timothy Leary urged. Our electric colors, flowing hair, fringes and groovy glasses rendered us most recognizable to each other, so disappearing into its colorful psychedelic rivers was relatively easy. The communes welcomed all, no questions asked; no police called. They offered warm welcomes, a harmonious environment, food and the hope that the world was as full of love as

---

[207] HIPPIE, Helper In Promoting Peaceful Individual Existence or Happy Individual Person Pursuing Individual Enlightenment (I never heard that during the 60's.)
[208] A street in San Francisco at the center of much of the Hippie activity of the 60's.

the movement claimed. The "free-love" slogan associated with Hippies meant one was free to have sex whether married or not and with the willing partners one met; however it was often misinterpreted by self-serving exploiters who decided it meant sexually uninhibited. That made hitchhiking for days on the Lincoln highway from New York to San Francisco even more dangerous.

Emboldened by the infinite invincibility, wisdom and foolishness of teens, many thumbed to the coast, confident, nothing could happen to them; although, there were rules of the road. Don't go high. Bring a blanket, snacks and water for long periods between cars; try to get dropped off at rest areas that will have food and a bathroom; keep a dime separate from the rest of your money to call someone in an emergency. And for the girls, go in pairs, a rule we couldn't always follow because both weren't always going to the same place. En Route to San Francisco, I had been with Hilda, but our paths separated when she went on to Sacramento. A few hours later, I was alone at a truck stop. No one was going to San Fran. Lunch time turned to dinner, but I continued to wait. Finally, a huge boat of a shiny panic-button read, two-door Buick Elektra sailed in front of me. "San Francisco?" I asked. They grinned, "Get in." The convertible top was up. As soon as they closed the door, I sensed I had made a mistake. The driver and his friend had the glazed, red eyes of stoners in the middle of a bender. The driver kept dropping his head down, so the car was weaving all over the road. They only spoke to each other, not to me, which was very odd. I don't recall all their words; I only remember the intense anxiety I felt; it escalated as I listened to them talk as if I wasn't there. The passenger asked the driver, "Think she's got any money?" In response, he shook his head. "Why'd you pick her up?" The driver glanced at me in the rear view mirror. "Hippie chick, you know? Fun." The passenger disagreed. "Naw man. I got my fun right here." Through the space between the seats, I watched as he wrapped an elastic tube around his arm before he shoved a needle into his vein. Emotional smoke signals of distress gusted off me to the Great Spirit. Nausea filled my belly and brought up a dry heave. The passenger's head fell forward and hit the dashboard. Almost immediately, the driver navigated the car to the side of the road.

"Hey, this is your stop Hippie girl," he barked and ordered his buddy to move forward to "Let her out!" Barely an instant after my shoe cleared the door, they sped off. I vomited on the side of the road and sat on my small bag. No one and nothing can ever bring me to believe anything other than the Great Spirit with his wise and mystical energy caused me to retch and make them stop. I didn't hitch. I walked in the hot sun for a long time; even though, cars pulled in front of me. I waved them on. Based on the number of people I knew to have hitched to San Francisco, I had assumed there would be a psychedelic, day-glow swath of dancing humanity streaming along the highway; there was not. The incident had shaken me out of my fantasy, and after these thousands of miles, I became aware of how naïve I had been. While walking and wondering if I could get there on foot, I saw another hitchhiker, a slim effeminate fellow with long, sun-bleached hair, sitting on up the road. His name was Don, a sixteen-year-old from Ohio who hoped to find, "A place where I can be me." He hemmed and hawed and opened his mouth.

"See that tooth?"

"The broken one?"

"Right. Talking to some shrink didn't cure me of liking boys, so my parents decided shock therapy would. It was torture."

I commiserated with him, and told him about having to hide my minority side and The Sheep and the Beats and wondered why he too didn't hide.

"I tried Then my mother walked in on me in a make out session with Scott. They're so fucked up, treating me like I'm sick. You're not sick because you're half, are you?"

"No, but I am not as smart as other people are."

"Don't you believe it sister. You seem plenty smart to me."

We consoled each other and decided to continue together. Only ten minutes later, we got a ride all the way to the corner of Haight and Ashbury. San Francisco was alive with the ebullient energy of throngs of untethered young people electrified with the thrill of being among those who thought similarly. Don and I discussed our options for sleep, should it be necessary. If the weather cooperated, we could sleep in the park. Otherwise, there's a place on Fell Street," he snapped his fingers to recall; "... the Switchboard and they have a system. They'll help us find a spot to crash," he said.

He had been there before with David, the heart he had left in San Francisco with whom he was hoping to reconnect. During the day, the park was an unholy Garden of Eden where the collective lot of HIPPIES came together. The ubiquitous appearance of feathers in everyone's hair was surprisingly unsettling to me. They had been attached, rather carelessly, and without the slightest regard for meaning. No harm done, but it caused me to think about how different groups of human beings assign different meanings to similar objects. For them the chicken feathers were adornment. My red-tailed hawk feather was for protection. Because it was unusual and beautiful people kept touching it, so I tucked it in my dress and instead wore a chicken feather dyed turquoise. Guitars and flutes broadcast our reveling, music loving, peace seeking, and often-nude presence amid the tropical green of Golden Gate Park.

LSD use was viewed by the mainstream as one of the most negative aspects of our sub-culture, but it wasn't just manufactured in the streets. The organic recipe had been turned into legal medication by the pharmaceutical company, Sandoz. In addition to psychiatrists giving it to their patients, they were taking it themselves. That's what I had heard. Neither Don nor I had tried it yet, but we wanted to and we were sure San Francisco held the ticket to this mind-expanding trip. We were certain we would find a "ticket" at the groovy Avalon Ballroom and, he hoped, his love. We arrived very early, so he could scope around for his friend. A super happy guy was handing out little Valentine's Day candies to everyone, and we slapped the candy from our palms into our mouths thinking our psychedelic trip was about to begin.

"Is this acid?" a guy asked.

I didn't hear the answer. About ten minutes while they were doing the sound check, big balloons of vivid color pulsed on the walls and ceilings and formed fascinating patterns, and I danced around the still unpeopled room in my bright yellow dress as freely as if I were alone at home. Apart from feeling as though I was a broken bit being tumbled around in a big kaleidoscope, I didn't experience anything. Disappointed I leaned on the stage. A man in striped pants strode over to the mic. Behind him was a small woman with shining eyes and long, messy, light-brown hair. She was swigging from an old brown jug. Like everyone, she beamed with happiness, though she was a little wobbly on her feet. The man said, "Testing one-two-.." but before he could say three, the woman took the mic and blasted a song out of her lungs with such gritty power that her whole body contorted as if exorcising demons. It was loud to me and a little scary, so I went outside. The psychedelic blobs vanished. I peeked back in and realized the valentine candy was just that and nothing more. The colors I had seen were a lightshow. Don was waving his arms to get my attention, so I went over to him.

"Here," he announced, "is your first trip," he said with his nose a few centimeters from mine. His pupils were as big as records. He handed me what appeared to be a tiny stamp. "Lick it."

"Did you already take yours?

He nodded and pushed my hand to my face. It had no taste.

"Whatever happens, meet in the parking lot at three am. Okay?" He looked me square in the face and added, "I don't want to lose you little girl."

Those words made me feel great, wanted. I didn't ask what the odd hour meant, and I don't think he would have known the answer anyway. He had become fascinated with his own hand. A well-tanned, blond-haired couple flung their arms in the air in a tribal dance and dropped them around Don. They writhed and rubbed their bodies against each other and lured me into their group grope dance. After a while, I was by myself trying to catch vivid flakes seemingly suspended in the air in front of me. My face ached, but I could not stop grinning. I was filled with an indescribable euphoria. I danced by myself, with one person and with many, all entranced, I assumed, by our hallucinations. Mine became sheets of day-glow rain falling around us. Suddenly a hand separated me from the crowd, and when we cleared the group, I saw it was an older man in his twenties.

"Your hair is far-out," he told me, and he buried his face in it which tickled. "Wanna go for a ride."

This sounded like the best idea I had ever heard in my life. I nodded. Nodding felt good. Walking felt good. Stretching my arms in the air felt good. Wiggling my hips felt good, so I did all of them as the man and I walked to his white Volkswagen convertible. I climbed in, and while he drove, I stood, and greeted everyone on the boulevard; they waved enthusiastically, and a few called back, "Have a nice trip," and "Far out man." The stars pulsed in the sky so brightly, I thought I could touch them, and I tried until we stopped. I jumped out and ran toward the sparkling expanse of ocean. He led me inside his house saying, "There are fewer bugs inside." It was a beautiful place right on the water. There was a bar and one whole wall held records from top to bottom, but he knew exactly which he wanted, one called, "Wild thing you make my heart sing." He handed me a drink, "Here. Apple brandy," took my hand and led me to a screened in porch.

I showed him the trails my hand was making, and he encouraged me to start from way above my head. When I did, he ran his hands firmly over my breasts and down the length of my waist which tickled. I pushed him away. So instead, he drew circles in my hand and they spiraled into the air. He collapsed on the couch and invited me to sit with him. Casually, he placed my fingers on his lap that felt unexpectedly soft and furry, so I looked and saw what I thought was a lifeless baby hamster. I screamed. He leapt up, and I saw it dangle just for a second before he tucked it inside and zipped his pants.

"What did you do to it?"

"To what?"

"That little hamster?"

Baffled and confused he asked, "What hampster?! What are you... You're tripping. There's nothing. Look," he said and held his arms out to the side.

I walked out to the cool ocean breeze beneath the moon. A few moments later he brought me a tumbler of water.

"That water is far out, just great," I told him beaming from ear to ear. "Thank you."

"You are even prettier when you smile. And this dress," he noted fanning the end playfully, and then asked, "How old are you?"

"I just finished the ninth grade," I told him proudly even though I hadn't.

Quite suddenly, he remembered he had to meet someone. Without turning out the lights or locking the house, we hopped back into the VW and drove to back to the Avalon. Reentering the ballroom, I recaptured part of my earlier high, but when I turned around, the man had disappeared. I was tired. I wandered into a quiet room full of statues and shadows of angels that reminded me of the angels that the flower scarf in Wes' room had made. And then my heart leaped. There was Wes. I ran across the room calling him, "Wes!" Tears ran down my face as I held him very tightly. "I knew you weren't dead. You just can't be."

"I could be anything for you baby but not dead."

That is not Wes' voice. I looked up to see a stranger. "Oh excuse me. I thought..."

"Sorry about your friend," he said and got lost among the crowd on the dance floor.

"There she is!" I heard Don shout and aw him striding toward me with a beautiful red-haired man he introduced as "David." Don wanted to know where I had been because he hadn't seen me, and he was worried. I loved hearing that he cared. I told them how I thought I had seen Wes. David and Don had each had a friend commit suicide; one drove his car off a cliff and the other deliberately overdosed. After we bowed our heads and sent positive energy to our departed friends, Don asked about the acid. I thought it was "okay, except for the man with the hamster in his pants." They giggled girlishly and then Don gave a brief explanation of hamsters. I shuddered in disgust.

"Yuk. I never want to see such an ugly thing again."

They laughed out loud, and Don said, "You may change your mind in a few years."

"Yes. One day, you won't be able to live without one," David concluded and exchanged a long meaningful kiss with Don.

David invited Don and me to stay with him on Laguna Street. I still had money from waitressing, but I had hoped to pad it with a new job. I didn't want to run out. However, it seemed I needed a social security card out there and a work permit which I vowed to get when I got back East. In late September, after a glorious and memorable summer dancing in the park, I decided it was time to return to Boston. Don stayed with David.

"You always have a place here," David told me on the way to the "Ride Board."

Getting out of San Francisco was much easier than getting in. The wall listed people who needed rides and those with cars who were willing to take them. There was usually an exchange for gas money, help or just company. Ava, the mother of a family with two kids saw me reading the listings and said I could ride with them all the way to Colorado and, "Maybe take care of the kids one night while Bill and I go out." I had to give pause for thought. When there were so many rides being offered, beggars could be choosers. I had to meet the children; they were five and seven, soft-spoken and adorable. I glanced around for their car. The road had taught me that very nice people can become crabby pretty fast in small, uncomfortable quarters, and Colorado was a couple of days away. I saw the biggest Volkswagen bus I had ever seen. She had to clear it with her husband who was packing the car.

"What girl?" he asked. She pointed to me. "Her, that Beat-Hippie Indian-looking chick? Awfully young Ava. Why is she out here all alone?"

She shrugged and hushed him, and they had a couple's talk that involved a lot of facial expression only they could interpret. In the end, I was welcomed aboard. Once in Yosemite and in the Fish Lake National Forest in Utah, we camped. Of all the road trips I have been on, this was one of the most spectacular. The idea of an intact family was foreign to me. Watching the children marvel at butterflies, rocks and trees with their parents made me a little sad. They asked me about my family, but I never really answered, just nodded and smiled. Everything went so well, they invited me to stay with them in Denver for a couple of days, but I had to get on with my little life. We all cried the day my friend, Bonnie, came and picked me up.

We went to a club called The Family Dog because her new "old man," as boyfriends were called, was an engineer and Lothar and The Hand People was playing.

"Doug this is my friend. She's been in San Francisco all summer," she laughed, "and she still hasn't done the deed with anyone.

When Doug jokingly volunteered his services, Bonnie slapped him playfully. "Are you crazy? She's a little girl."

"Not that little," he noted staring at my fully developed bosom.

I read somewhere that Betty Davis said, she had felt sexy from the moment she was six, "And let me tell you it was hell, sheer hell, waiting to do something about it." I had no such urges. Unlike Miss Davis, I was more than prepared to wait, but I was still hurt by Bonnie calling me a "little girl." Ha. I looked as mature as she did, and *I've been at all night parties with hip poets in dark glasses, musicians and artists. For crying out loud, I had hitched to San Francisco, tripped on acid, saw Wes return from the dead and hung out on in Golden Gate Park and Haight. What's she done?*

Backstage at the Dog, stagehands hustled to and fro oblivious to me, and then there was no one; I was alone. A young man with a mane of light brown locks walked in and paced in wobbly hops of heel-toe-nervousness. I looked down and back; he was gone. I closed my eyes and thought about going outside, but I knew if I went out, I wouldn't be able to get back in without a ticket. Bonnie's old man had brought us in through the back. Suddenly, there was a tug on a few strands of my hair, a gesture that had been an invitation to fight in grammar school, and it caused me to tense and expect the worst. Over my shoulder, I saw the heel-toe walker. He had a shy, child-like aura. The side of his mouth curved into a smile. His breathing filled the space between us with the unpleasant vapors of booze that I hated, but at that moment, I didn't mind. Gravity let me go, and my whole body was filled with the sensation of floating, and a pleasurable, tingling; it was exciting. I felt my ancient Native soul slumbering within awaken and peer through the window of my eyes into his. It saw a similar peering back from within his eyes. Glittering Tinkerbelle-like fairy dust showered in the air where, for a nanosecond, the two immortal celestial entities within us wafted together in a spiritual union. *This must be what love feels like,* I decided, and *one day I will find this with a human someone.* When the beings retreated into us, he came into view, his soft face, his large liquid pupils spilling into his blue-green irises. His little half smile mischievously leaped onto my mouth. The mesmerism was daunting and had made me a little nervous. I simply could not avert my eyes, so I jerked my head toward my shoes and ran my hand over the soft suede. I could feel his eyes on me. A moment later, he buried his hand in my hair and mussed it up, yet another reminder I was just a kid. A voice hollered out, and he strode away. The force of his leaving drew me to my feet. He paused, glance over his shoulder and smiled with both sides of his mouth.

Bonnie and her old man returned in a grand rumple of their velvet, denim and leather clothes in what I guessed to be a post-coital glow. "Your face is all red. What happened?" Bonnie asked as we observed the crowd and the stage from the wings. Doug directed us down the stage steps to the front of the house. Heel-toe walker appeared on the stage and the audience erupted into a cacophonous roar of welcome. "Jim!" a few people called. "Is everybody in?" he asked. "Yeah!" they bellowed. After a couple of organ notes, he sang. "Light my Fire." I did feel like a kid when I realized he was a big musician and I hadn't even recognized him. I hoped I had not hurt his feelings. As it is with performers, he was in another universe onstage. He morphed into a seemingly overly intoxicated narcissist dramatically lurching and writhing with somewhat clumsy seductiveness on the stage.

About a year later, I heard the same song on the radio. In interviews, he claimed it was not he but the ancients who occupied his body that gave rise to his legendary jumping, screaming. No one knows what perpetuated his constant drinking and overindulgence in drugs. On the wings of his mysterious personality and considerable talent, he flew to the sun but a little too close. Next thing the world knew, in 1971, the wreckage of the star Jim Morrison nee "James Douglas Morrison" was abandoned and washed up, on the cold and desolate shores of a marble Parisian bathtub. (RIP).

❀ ❀ ❀

By then, the counter-culture had lost Janis Joplin, Jimi Hendrix and Brian Jones. In fact, three years earlier, the Hippie scene itself had been declared dead. With it went my childhood and the unknown person I could have been had I grown up only among Sheep.

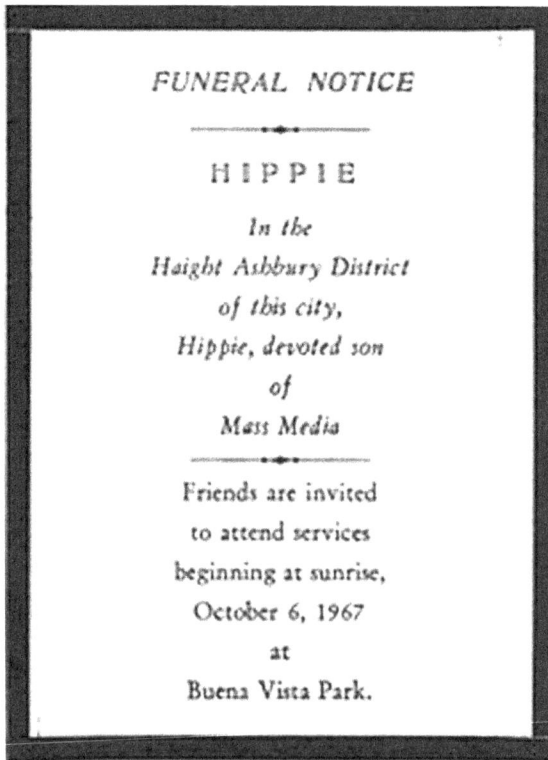

FUNERAL NOTICE

H I P P I E

*In the
Haight Ashbury District
of this city,
Hippie, devoted son
of
Mass Media*

Friends are invited
to attend services
beginning at sunrise,
October 6, 1967
at
Buena Vista Park.

Beat Hippie Poetry

Depression was my muse when it came to poetry. Quite a few of the following were written in the midst of my worst depressions. I was surprised I was able to write anything in that state. Oddly, I have not been inspired to write a poem since.

What follow are those for which others have expressed appreciation or fondness. I didn't know how else to choose.

© "Heel-Toe Walker" drawing by Winchinchala 1965

Morrison's Silhouette

Light
How powerful its absence
silhouetting a young man,
at once summoning his music,
his words, the dreams and desires of a decade
thoughts daring and defiant
spiritual, death, poetry, inquiring.
How powerful light; its absence
delineating a man, a neglected child
bounding poetic disconnected

into a sexy, cool hip world
up-ended in the power of flower
petals spelling rebellion in
jingling beads and peace signs
promising free love
in a splash of news shocking,
lewd, lusting for love
stalked by a feast of virgins
and the souls of dead Indians.

How powerful light;
its absence
dimming a brightly
lighted midnight
somewhere.
Somewhere?

Somewhere silhouetting the young man
instantly recognizable as
a poet, a generation, a myth.
His agony trivialized.
His dreams and songs romanticized
While his true life is
raunchy and debauched
unsung, unresolved, unrealized.
Now his life is a powerful light
burning brightly somewhere
somewhere else.

Rainy day Funeral
(For "Wes")

From high cottony-grey clouds
your celestial tears shower
and shimmer on lush green trees
rustling out a song over your grave.
Your always-absent father is present
suddenly smaller huddled next to
your mother mooning ghostly pale.
beneath enormously grievous
black umbrellas held down low

above their shared sorrow, guilt
and shame for not having known
or not having asked you if you needed help
or how to ask if you had said...yes.

Classmates' anguished and frightened faces
bow over their mourning black and
their young arms embrace each other
in consolation among the heavenly scent of
—you can't imagine—how many flowers
brought by neighbors and relatives close
and distant, showing up, proving they did care,
now, what does it matter?

What cruel evil blinded you,
put your head in a noose &
loosed your weight to gravity and Hell
in the presence of
the dog who loved you unconditionally?
It killed me too spiritually,
trapped a piece of my soul
in the sinews of your remains
in the plush crushed red velvet
of your casket immediately recognizable
as expensive, carved mahogany
your parents' evidence of love
for all to see at the funeral home
and where but angels would
once in the ground... eternally.

Mr. Know it All

(For Bob)

Mr. Know it All
didn't know it all.
He was worshipped
because he knew everything.
But he didn't know
the one last thing
he needed to know to be
"all knowing" and
he didn't want to know it
because he knew he would
go insane
knowing it all.
So he ran away from his inner self
by skulking his outer self
in designer label men's wear
and striking GQ poses
in intercontinental hotels
where each week they changed the
menu's international dish and
the costume of the
garcon-ober-waitress
transporting him
1000 leagues around the world
from the blasé café chair
no seatbelt, no film, no destination
but "fat city"
for the already vacationing owner
who raised the minimum to $5.00
which all who were "in the know,"
agreed was fair fare to sit there.

And sitting there
in a cache of smoke
in the interlude between
Hungarian goulash and French Pastry
the final mortal blow of knowledge
simply crossed his mind
transforming him into
an enlightened maniac
who took the check and gave the waitress this tip,
"Do yourself a favor. Stay stupid beautiful."

Times Square

The neon sun – blue, red, yellow
flickering fragmented spelling
words and shapes and beings overhead
casts its dim rays on the night owls
flying out of the underground smoking
in search of food for their souls
wearing berets, not wearing berets
their jackets and top buttons undone.
Shapely chicks hair fluttering
tattered sails catching all they can
in the dingy, dinty din down under out in the open
guiding them along the invisible paths of good times
outside of Hayes' Bickford's & Girlie Shows,
music shops' windows with the
quiet instruments lonely in the neon sun
flashing repeatedly brightly on the mouth of
the jazz club across the way with the musicians
belching blue notes blues blare there
interrupted by yellow trumpets in some
hot mambo red-
heads, blondes and brunettes, the chicks
have all forgotten their girdles and look cool
blue eyes, brown, maybe green beneath dark glasses.
Their powdered faces and their black clothes
are canvases for the man-made neon sun
is a Picasso

in the night painting innumerable borderless
not-so-abstract abstracts all over
making newspapers black and white illegible
to tired late night workers
out of habit by passing by the fabricated day
shuffling into the dinty dingy din
down under forty second street
annoyed by the festive daytime scene above
whores' legs
visible to their high thighs
invite them, invite anyone
with cash.
Blue splashes on taxis
"Eat at Joe's" "All nude" "All Night" "Nemo's" signs
catch some bodies speeding safely away from
their class routine,
the usual opera scene
in top-hats and tuxes
in limos and taxis spreading time-lapsed yellow
stripes though the bright, smoky night-peopled portrait.
         Times Square

Summer

Summer is a 3-D color thing
a singing swinging 90 day happening
hundreds of shapes and shades
smooth and casual talkers
unhurried languid walkers
parasol topped sidewalk hawkers
overheated toddler squawkers
people and people and more
shopping in the malls
enjoying the sporadic zephyrs
moving to the music from
convertibles, fine cruisin' cruisers
part of the 3-D color thing happening outside
Summer is people and people and more
forgetting modesty in
short shorts and halters
tank tops, t-straps and T's
bare thighs, shapely shoulders
backs and love handled middles
responsive nipples on body fruit:
peaches, grapefruits and melons
taste best air conditioned
sucked in the shade of the trees
or the white hot sun by the sea.
The sea gulls swooping on sandwiches
children's gleeful screaming solos
above the chorus of the ocean's waves
chased from the shore by unwitting dogs
trampling down sandcastles

attempting to catch Frisbees
red, yellow, blue: cabana stripes
polka dots, primary color swirl
a fabulous frostee, lick a softee
have a frozen coffee, sip minty ice tea
feel the hat, breathe the humidity
hear the musical harmony played
by roller blades an' skateboards, bikes' spokes
Summer is energy, also lovely lazy
Summer is a 3-D color thing
a singing, swinging, 90 day happening.

Life's no Music Video

Life's no music video
dull bits taken out
highlights spliced together
side by side
syncopating the gentle
petal to blossom
blooming of events
to the blur of a pinwheel
on a rainy day.
Life's the action following though
in clamor accented silences
to a million possible endings
with the slow passing of real time
thoughts are thoughtlessly spoken
words don't rhyme.
we don't move in slow motion
no violins play for love's emotion
tender touches, lips on cheeks
confessed feelings;
no trumpets blare for the hurried rush
flared anger, fists on tables,
regrettable shoutings;
no sambas punctuate jaunty gaits
playful eye contact, flirtatious glances
moonlit beach walks.
No saxes blow for sad good-byes.
blue moods, suppressed feelings.
Life's the action following through.
Life's no music video
dull bits taken out
highlights spliced together
side by side

Real time often passes so slowly
that it spins and flips backwards
even boredom becomes exciting.
Everyone is not well-dressed
seen at their best
in a series of soft-focused
best moments from great angles
for everyone else to see
in a montage of sexy desirable poses
of success and unattainability
We look lousy when we wake up
And sometimes for days after that.
Love is declared to the deaf,
uncaring ears
we have all carried in our pockets
on at least one occasion
Lovers break each others hearts
to their favorite song.
They kiss others to it too,
behind closed doors in madding show places.
Rarely are the sets for life's dramas
tinted misty violet, rose-blue
It's 75-100-150 watts, maybe shaded.
It's fluorescently unflattering,
starkly sunlit, dimly overcast and dark.
Life's sets dim and brighten in
the rolling ebb of light...
washed out in too much, faded in too little,
imperfect, unpredictable, uncontrollable,
Life's no music video.

Box of Stars, Box of Moonlight

(For Yianni)

They're gazing at you;
they're wishing on me
Night's nothing but flat
black without us
So I'm waiting in a doorway
slowly fading of sun
Waiting softly for you to
come

Cuz you've got a box of
moonlight
And I've got a box of stars

for the sky approaching indigo
Indigo Indigo Indigo Indi-
gone
We are the lights
We'll make it bright
We'll make it right
The nights are our days!
We're stealing; we're streaming
we're shooting right into the
dark
breaking through pains
in shafts and rays on windows.

You'll dance on steel guitar
strings
Me with naked sweaty
shoulders sweetly
on the bar
from far so close
bursting white glare in the
mirror

I tingle with high anticipa-
tion
Because everything is nothing
without us

Night's nothing but flat
black.
So I wait in the doorway
slowly fading of sun
Smiling
Cuz you've got a box of
moonlight
And I've got a box of stars

Yes, you've got a box of
moonlight
And I've got a box of stars
a box of stars; a box of stars,
a box of stars.

Sexy

Sometimes sad is Sexy—very Sexy
and sometimes Sexy is sad.

Good Morning by Winchinchala, 01/ 01/ 1980

Nipple Erections

Nipple erections are possible
when temperatures are up and
fish-net shirts are in
on carefully coppered nubiles
tottering and mincing by
snapping and blowing bubbles
between glistening and glossy lips
yakking and reacting on Soaps
with vacant but noisy interest
giggling and grinning about HIM
with lustful, yearning young eyes
when he passes by to his car
idling high on octane attention
emitting the fumes of

smoking rock music.
Nipple erections are visible
but only to passers-by

when the nubiles move together
wondering why he didn't notice
They squirm and come together
as a single sensuous creature
with female fluffy falling hair
on six skittish colt's legs.

Ineluctable

light kisses  soft laughter

affectionate   exalted   nakedness
caressing pleases. Nerves:
tighten & release
tighten & release tighten & release
tighten & release tighten & release
reprieve
breathing rapidly shallow
senses heightened
spark   electric
musky vapors & mounds steam
stem & flower
bloom in heat
sternums
sliding  colliding
over heart beats
sweet sweat droplets
on foreheads & shoulders
under bangs colored nutmeg tickle &
catch

on lashes. Desirous
        lips swollen
            wrap around grins
             &
      loose   tongues   delight
masculine-féminine
        féminine—masculine
        pelvises
        parry
  pro--------lon-------ging

        playing eclipsed   by
          arriving lust

♩ = 130   rhythmic beats

    rapture
        ineluctable

Fish Monger © Segar

Fish Fillay

He loved shopping at her fish market
spending thousands of seconds looking
spending himself dry, again and again
until happy exhaustion
brought her chestnut awning
cascading down in front of her eyes.

She loved to watch him shopping
losing his mind over fish slowly
admiring and contemplating
sniffing, ~ taking his time,
fondling this,
licking that ~
sampling without asking
glistening dark pink, flesh

and though cloyed, he would
finally giving her all her had
for one last piece of fresh raw fillay.

Sinner, Sinner

sinner sinner...

sinner on a
bed of flames
licking at my flesh
burning with desire
temptation and urges
spark a pyre
fantastically
inextinguishable.

Who knew what a blaze
our match would ignite
an ardent sinner
long disregarded
a sinner secreted in you
awakening ravenous
firm and naked in the night.

Tinder sparking,
luminous tongues
lapping
dancing red
stroking me
along my torso
gloriously
from limb to limb to limb

sinner sinner...
sinner on a
bed of flames
thrashing
on instinct
wordless
tireless
sinner gone insane
kindling the devil
in infernal passions
over and over again
incinerating romance,
yet
lasciviously amorous.
We combust
in a roaring
blaze of lust.

Reborn

I was dying while living
almost unconscious
until the music
of your black cowboy boots
and your big brains
oozed down on me
and woke me up
with some song you wrote.
Listening to you
singing sweetly, screaming
their melodies softly
while reading books
you placed in my hands
referring me to Alan Watts
and Jim Morrison of years ago
denying Christ, embracing sexuality.

I came to realize
I am living while dying
for more music to pour
down on me
arouse me ethereally
from this drowsy winter still life
to abet an orgasm of Spring
slip me off my seat to
rise me up on tippy toe for
your mouth mine to melding
into the universe.

Your body mine to thrill with an
infusion of fluid stars,
I am fully conscious, alert now
Helplessly nestling you
comfortably unfamiliar delectable
and doing a new harmonizing
Please!   Don't!   Stop!
Please! Don't! Stop!
Drench me, soak me, drown me
in your milky way.
Slaked, satisfied, finished.
Dust to dust
thoughts of dying
vanquished by lust
and the music of black cowboy boots,
I am hanging crazy from your shadow
I am not dying;
I am not living;
I am reborn

Il Dictatore

I.

He was in the army,
Ill Dictatore in the sexual revolution
uniformed in an old black sweater
and tight leather pants
right next to the skin
of his sinewy legs that
ran straight and narrow
and strong right up to
his face, angular and experienced.
A platoon of girls and women knew
the cool of his golden peace sign
slid back and forth across
his chest and kissed the words
free and love tattooed
on his upper thigh.
He was an army of one
deployed by Satan to
carry out his erasure
of missionary sex
to liberate the world from
sexual inhibition and carnal ennui.
His very gate was a moving violation.

II

Il Dictatore touched with fingers
but first grabbed with his scent,
lured with his gaze all at once
shocking and awfully arresting
led to a trial and sentencing of
bodies to an undetermined
time together with candles and
a bottle of wine in quarters comfy
as he commenced his mission
smiling wryly and in one motion
pulling his sweater over his head
lathering his hands with lotion
and gently plucking and
kissing timidity and modesty
from erogenous zones writhing
around.

III

Dictatore presented his own.
The peace sign beat visibly with
the throbbing of his heart
while he examined his eager recruit
lying trembling in a quiet as audible
as a thousand people listening for
the sound of a falling star

The Official Sexy Solitary Suicide
Girl

slim, pretty coquette
winsome, mirthful girl
radiating youth from
the toes of wobbly new stilettos
to an everywhere glancing head
cascading hair around your face,
flipped casually over your shoulder
inexperienced fingers dipped in red
slide down your ribs to your waist
and rest on your inchoate hips turning
swiveling you along.
the room is intoxicated with
the dew of your exuberant elixir
cast unconscious in naked coyness
your playful available flirt
too loudly delivered, at once forgiven
by the grace of your elegant arms
and charmingly goofy guffaw
as you stumble and try to look smooth.

linger near, linger here,
let me undress you with my eyes
and run my fingers over the contour
of your tantalizing naïveté
and supple silhouette responding
in the obscene raunch of my mind
but don't unbutton your cloak
with the cherry red lining or empty its
pockets of their complications.
inflate me

with your flashing eyes and attentive airs
lead me on with your hand pressed and
on my chest over my racing heart,
violate my space with your breath
speak coyly, soft so close to my face
that your eyelashes whisper on my cheek;
then offer up some vigorous "Hey" to
some someone over there
and saunter freshly away
just saunter freshly away.

Two Strings to Her Bow

Ode to Flirtin'

Fancifree flirtin'
a thing to do.
And if I had my druthers
we'd never get to know one another
me and you.
We'd forever just meet in bars
along the Avenue
Not have to—Not must to
Just happen to
whenever we have the time.
For fancifree flirtin's
a thing to do.
No porcelain passions
for me and you.
No broken promises.
No tears to dry
only you and I
perfunctorily, painlessly playfully
doing nothing muching
about getting closer together.
Just fancifree flirtin' a thing to do.
And if I had my druthers,
and I think I do,
we'd never get to know one another
me and you.
And we'll have a perfect relationship
never ending,
never having begun.
Fancifree flirtin's
harmless grown-up fun.

~ ~ ~

Solitary

~ ~ ~

"The loneliest moment in someone's life is when they are watching their whole world fall apart, and all they can do is stare blankly."

— F. Scott Fitzgerald, *The Great Gatsby*

Window Friends
©Winchinchala 1971

Loneliness

loneliness will pour liquor
down your throat
and sit you next to people
who talk louder
than you like to talk
...about anything:
politics, food or cinema
though clearly, they don't
even like film
or maybe they do,
but they haven't seen
the same flicks as you.
So talk leads to weather,
the price of fuel and rent and all
So loneliness sticks.

And keeps on sticking
with you though
you are with others
on a long commute
not home or work
but at the library or
in a store
a block or
a day or just an hour away.

It plays hide and seek
on the busy streets
and crowded buses
just as much as it does
on a cushion at home
on the too roomy sofa
or an empty chair
across a big kitchen table
no longer set for two

or even one.

Placemats go
by the computer monitor
or the coffee table
in front of the TV light
blathering, brilliantly
obscuring loneliness
which had you pen names
in your phone book.

They are strangers
who try to remember you
when they receive
your holiday greeting card
and loneliness puts
a photo of your alter ego
on some webpage somewhere
where the bored and abject,
insecure and highfalutin flicker
as fantastic in cyberspace
as they once were stoned
in a room brimming with limbs
and faces fractured in the mirrors
of a disco ball.

loneliness leads you to thinking
dogs you talk to are not annoyed
by your intrusion on their thoughts of
dropped steak tips, and romps through
fields of long-ago buried bones.
But they seem to understand
your desire to run away
to the circus or any
peopled destination,
even if it's just the coffee shop

on any corner
where in foamy faux-lattéd
company
loneliness can at least
be briefly dispatched
to cower in the
dark, linty corners of
hems and sleeves and pockets
hopefully to forget
but most likely to wait for you:
-loneliness-

Footsteps

The echoing clomp of unawaited
footsteps in a tile hallway
shuffle in front of a door
and are greeted by the kiss
and scent of no one
the aroma of nothing cooking
a lorn finger on a switch scatters
away the unpeopled darkness
a sigh unheard escapes
from the person unexpected and invisible
whose eyes glance at the
unringing telephone
whose ears hear no requests
for dinner.
Dinner
the fork not even accompanied
by a knife
clinks out a disconsolate
dinner tune
on the porcelain plate
and later on, there is
unshared laughter at
a sitcom and tuts
over the evening news
before the echoing stomp
of the footsteps on a parquet floor
are muffled in a carpet.

Loners

Each one admitted to the other
"I am a loner,"
One out loud
the other muttered
to the floor.
One a loner by fear
the other by choice
two loners two-gether

Two loners are not one.
Can't be.
One and one is two,
Always,
Never one.
Two in one room
At times are close as
Two, 6 thousand miles apart.
Sad soul searchers
voyeurs of others
they know no one
Unless one is a loner.
It takes one to know one.

Each one said to the other, "Good-bye,"
One out loud
The other muttered
to the window pain and they parted
never having really met.

Lonely traveler
in a lonely universe

Lonely traveler
in a lonely universe
sliding your celestial
body sublime along mine
trying to slake your thirst
for touch, for closeness
for notice, corporeal divine
trying to reciprocate pleasure
no way to measure success
pressing so close pushing so
nearly
suffocating me with
your comfortable weight

yet we are still as far apart as
two lonely travelers in
this lonely universe,
the horizonless vastness
dwarfing we two bright stars
barely visible flecks of light
luminous you and luminous me
collide and we subside
breathing one breath as you
traverse the landscape of my sternum
imbued with passion's dew

our hearts as close as violet to blue
on any given rainbow
our motion gyrating
our bodies
into the firmament, undulating
a mixed ecstasy cocktail cream
yet still
we orbit separately
we lonely travelers
through the
vast horizonless infinity
of a lonely universe..

Wedding Ring
Slipped of my Finger

Warm and sweet and young
were we feathered amorous two
murmuring, trilling, cooing,
as lovey dovey lovebirds do,
when we, with golden rings
that fit us perfectly,
married us in June,
then roosted high on a hillside
near the vivacious, scintillating, sun
and the soothing, whispering moon
to feed our burgeoning love
through our many windows.

Citing the calm of dark
And desire for privacy
you preferred them closed,
covered with heavy curtains,
I had only hung for
color and effect,
not muffling our laughter
and music or the conflicts
that ensued over
prohibiting the view
of exactly what we had wanted:
the stream, the deer, the sky,
in nature's sanctuary
where other lovebirds
flew playfully freely,
as should have we
as could have we,
had the windows been opened.

Had the windows been opened
each of us could have soared off
to explore our individuality
see what we could see and grow
to miss each others company,
forever to return to hillside us
where duets not yet written
waited our composition
where phrases not yet formed
waited to be spoken
in a home illuminated by
celestial day and night lights
freshened with air and freedom
not shackled by golden rings
fitting too loosely now
so loosely
mine slipped off my finger and
wrapped around my throat
inhibiting sustenance to my soul
that should have been waxing
with yours.

Green girls blue are golden

Nursing drinks
riding barstools
the way they used to
Daddy's shoulders
green girls are playing games
unchaperoned
watched by
their mothers' warnings
they mind
their manners
are in the way
at the game of chance
in the recreation room
of the night school of experience
answering "yes," mischievously
short-sheeting their own beds
by doing the boy's next door
for a laugh
crying when the fable's end
is sad
not happy
as it was when
Gramma read it

for the last of countless times
7300 evenings ago
when life first began
imitating art
now found untrue
from a philosophical point of view
discovered at the bottom of drinks
bought by possible next men
last seen on the last page
somewhere near
 "...happily ever after."
Green girls blue are golden
drowning mothers' voices
the barstool wanders off the path
and the fable
forgotten
ENDS

Anticipating

It's 10 before gleeful o'clock
when he will be here.
I'll sit. I'll stand. No sit.
I'll change my blouse.
See me smile to

15 after gleeful to worried o'clock.
When will he be here?
By the window.
Did I hear the door?
Oh the article. Where is the article to share?
See me searching to please to
Half past worry rings doubtful O'clock
that he is coming here.
Watch must be fast. Call the time.
What day is today?
Oh is that the phone?
Didn't it ring?
See me wait to

17 minutes later, panic
and self degradation o'clock
strike when he isn't here.
Phone sitting presents an oral dilemma
to smoke, to eat, to drink. (I don't drink!)
to think "Something happened," to

Half past a second hour, crying o'clock
when He hasn't called and definitely isn't here.
Go alone. He might call. Stay.
I'll change my blouse.
I'll redo my nail.
Fix my unmussed hair.
Pick up the phone to call.
Feel pride stop me.
See me watch the news to

12 and ridiculous O'clock
when he obviously isn't coming
and the anchorman's woeful look
seems just for me.
See me feign apathy, then sleep to
Ring. Ring. Ring. Ring. Ring. Ring. Ring.
He's calling no doubt.
I won't answer. The damn jackass
"Hello? Who?" Yes it's me.
"No I was not sleeping. No it's not too late.
I'll be there." See me internalize
                              See me hate myself?

Old Man on Tremont Street

Won't get to eighty-four
in ten days
with you sneakin' up on me
like that girlie.
Used to be an old man
didn't have to look around.
Nobody did.
It's all different now.
Used to be, we'd sit out in those old chairs
the wooden foldin' ones by the stoop
Smoke a Havana cigar til it
was a firefly on Tremont Street.
Kennedy put out them lights
with the Bay-O-Pigs.
Put up these big 'lectric ones

Yes sir, me and my boys
we was the eyes of the night.
Knew what was what,
what was nothin' and
whowas goin' where.
Said, "evenin'" to the woman
in the window hopin'
for men droppin' by
heads down, wearin' hats,
collars up, they'd stroll in
but hustled out.
Real quiet we'd watch 'em

or lovers meetin'
under that big ol' tree
getting' and givin' kisses
times real long
in steamy heat
and frigid cold.
Don' matter none.
we grinned ear to ear
cause we'd all been there too
out under the moon
without mama knowing
or maybe the wife.
And we'd laugh outloud
at the couple upstairs
scrappin' like cats and dogs.
once she threw skillet
right through the window
bounced off my buddy's toe.

He died in the war,
a lot of 'em did
or their hearts gave out
you know.
Now it's just me
Don't sit on the stoop no mo'.
can't get up so good.
That's all right.
I still see what's going where.

Like you girlie.
by yo'self
back and forth
everyday
rushing to John Hancock's[209]
Pretty girl like you
can do better
'n that cold, guy.
Give you more 'n pocket change
Give him up!
He's eatin' up your youth
Swallowin' your time
Indigestin' you whole
Getchu a flesh and blood man or
where, you always
be all alone.

Hey?
Who Dat?
I won't get to eighty-four in ten days
with you folks sneakin' up
on me.
Hey girlie.
I see ya there.
Hey, have a nice day, Ya hear?

---

[209] The John Hancock Life Insurance building in Boston, Ma.

~ ~ ~

Suicide

~ ~ ~

Warning: These are quite dark. I wanted to throw them away. My friend John suggested: "Keep them. Or even, get them out there. You might want to share, in case there are a few who feel just like you but can't express it." Made sense, but it was hard not to destroy them.

The Small Side of Paradise

For Joy

Misunderstood.
Lonely.
unhugged by a father,
untouched by a mother
who ran into the damn gas oven
with the sleepy, brindled cat,
the saddest person was Joy.
Or was she the angriest?
A flame from something
ignited a hot black fire
in her once vivacious
light green eyes... glowing vacant.
No firemen coming to her rescue
foamed frothy cocktails down her throat.
They were but dew drops on an inferno
bellowed by vodka tonics
enraging the fire in her core
melting moments of glad youth
like her lover's wartime farewells
and their gleeful running-back-again hellos.

Portraits of her own children
fuel the fiery tongues
flaming out her mouth in
obscenities scorching everyone
even herself
Screaming hot.
A blaze that was ablaze in depressing agony
When no firemen came to her rescue
she placed one last booze bottle on her mouth
and sucked in success
dousing the fire, ending the pain
and washing her own remains
onto the small side of paradise.

Tragic Impulse

To a victim from a survivor

My dear friend
who shared so much with me:
despondent tales of childhood,
casual encounters, playing concerts
New York to Paris to Vienna,
where you eagerly succumbed
to ardent love's mercurial ways
with a "titled aristocrat,"
La de da de da
He was a tenor who delighted
in pieces written in minor keys
whose enthusiastic affections
your yearning-heart read as
a dream-come-true,
a romantic Sibelius symphony
but time revealed it
a Beethoven Bagatelle[210].
The drama of your unpredictable tears
over him, your lovers, your mother
sad films and books or a dinner
you cooked imperfectly
come to mind with
raindrops now pattering
on grey headstones,
rainbowed umbrellas
black cars' hoods,
and peri-autumnal leaves
causing them to weep as I,
large the tears, I wish could
cleanse the final perverse image of you
slumped in the bath tinted red

---

[210] A light, short piece of music.

with your blood
overflowing and flooding
the tile floor
where wrong-headed
you left this world,
left behind
your naked body
was so pale,
your talented graceful hands
eerily lifelike on your chest
the right twisted and clasped
rigidly around your bloodied left
as if a last minute change of heart
tried to dam the flow
from the raw, craggy slashes,
inflicted, well...not by you,
my dear friend
full of wit and vim
music and love
but by the sudden tragic impulse
that undammed your rivers of life
too quickly,
too savagely
too completely
for your sensibilities to stem.

Radio Radio Belial[211]

This is Radio Radio Radio Belial.
This is the last transmission
coming to you from
the bottom of a bottomless glass
in the basement of a timeless place
there is no light, no space, no air
everyone is loaded, a single shot
unhappy bullet, anxious in a chamber
a bottle to the lips, mouthful of pills,
blade to the scars on the scars of the wrist
standing on a box, a rope round the neck
encircled black lines around the eyes
drawn wider and darker still by
insomnia, confusion,

Reality appears up side down, turned around.
like a dizzying reeling phantasmagoria,
snake-charming breasts jiggling and
sheathed sequined bottoms sparkling
promoting pornographic thinking
slurping pig-out pastry buffets bar
spin-the-wheel-n-win fortunes guaranteed
flashing electric across sinful Vegas skies
a haze of cocktail vapors glow red sunset
silhouetting small chapel-crossed horizons
from dusk to dawn stimulating mercilessly
from dawn to dusk all the glitz and glam
whisked off by brilliant bristles of desert sun
reveal the Garden of Eden a restaurant
closed indefinitely for renovations
All is but an oasis, a wily mirage, just sand
not reality—not Life.

---

[211] Belial, a Biblical name for the devil.

Life?
Life is the fire and brimstone.
The apocalypse is in the street.
The apocalypse is at the door
The apocalypse is in your soul
Pull the trigger!
Drink the drink!
Swallow the pills!
Kick the box!
Plunge the steel.
Let lose your red rapids of blood
to crash the seawalls that
stemmed receipt of comfort and joy
silenced bells and love and merry things.

Launch into death's depths unknown;
shun lingering fears of the dark;
unrequited conversation,
unaccompanied consternation;
vanquish hurt lavished by life
perish the terror of inferiority
pull
drink
swallow
kick
plunge.

This is Radio Radio Radio Belial.
This is the last transmission
coming to you from
the bottom of a bottomless glass
in the basement of a timeless place
no light.
no space.
no air.

Seven-Letter Word

SIREN screaming
dogs barking
tires thudding over pot holes
commercial blaring
inaudibly
person walking hurryingly
expected nowhere
book thumping
on the floor
floating, floating
floating away
breathing
not breathing
breathe.
breathe.
Breathe is
a seven-letter word like:
Capture
Rapture
Ecstasy
Suicide
Thought.
thinking
nagging
ghosting
conniving inner monologue
Suicide
never uttered

in context
but whispered.
ever after
it is a foggy
cat-pawed
phantom
a seven letter word:
Unheard
Screamed
on a page
between dusk and twilight
in inexplicable darkness
and unbearable pain
to silence
isolation? loneliness?
No!
Who knows?
maybe this is just
apathy ~ life fatigue
Sadness has seven
Breathe!
Breathe
inhale, two, three
exhale four, five, six
seven-gulp breathe
hurts like Hell
disfigures
victimizes

That's the power of
a seven letter word
SUICIDE
carefully penned
angrily crumpled up
or discarded unread
too despised
to view
one thinks the act
selfless not selfish
misunderstood
suicide
a seven letter word
like
Silence
like
Release
Freedom
Like
Goodbye. . .

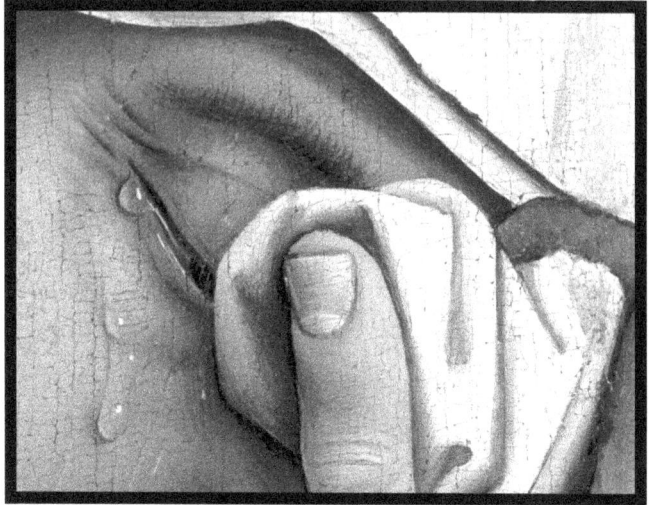

How to Perform a Depressionectomy

a human hollow full of dark
lost in the winter summer park of life,
sandy white and snowy bright
invisible in a forest of isolation:
loud bluebells silently ringing;
anguish writhing black internally;
sorrow eats away at life unrelentingly,
gradually, painfully.
How to perform a depressionectomy?

A hug or kiss from someone dear
or the sight of a clumsy puppy
perhaps a glad glimpse of sun,
shining through a leafy green canopy
a room with an ocean view?
lunching on arugula?
shopping? shopping for shoes,

talking to friends,
listening to their good news?
These just treat the symptoms temporarily.

Build a damn across inexplicable woes
with lithium pebbles or
infuse the river blue with liquid Prozac
performs a depressionectomy, but
inevitably the river dilutes it,
so dark today becomes dark tomorrow,

Is there no match for melancholy
mercilessly, metastasizing?
Little by little it will consume me
become me until
until killing it means killing me.
I must think...
I must think...
How to perform a Depresionechtomy?

The Official Sexy Solitary Suicide

Farewell note: # 1

The weight of black
        the dimming of light
        the sense of loss
            of love and joy
              of waking
leave me in so much pain
      in the dark that
           the loss of life feels like the only way out.
           Running didn't work
           Working didn't work
           Medicating didn't work
           Drinking didn't work
           Reading didn't work
           Sleeping didn't work
           TV didn't work
           Talking didn't work
           nothing can make IT go away
              Please stop trying.
  the weight of black
        the dimming of light
        the sense of loss
            of love and joy
              of waking
it came from no where
one day or one night
without warning
crashing violently
     through logic and reason
         and abducted the essence of me
             replacing it with malignant grief
rendering me blind to sunrises
      embracing the dark;
           letting go of life
              feels like the only way out

of alienation, loneliness
and the sorrow.
Running didn't work
Working didn't work
Medicating didn't work
Drinking didn't work
Reading didn't work
Sleeping didn't work
TV didn't work
Talking didn't work
as either a diversion or antidote

for dark, black thoughts.
aphorisms extolling the power of
the positive and hope
are administered with the best of intentions
and quell them as well as
whipped cream
can
the blues
be cured because you want it to be?
by incessantly suggesting
herbal remedies or eastern philosophies,
new age shrinks and omega-3?
All that cheering spotlights
the tragedy of a person in
the ravenous mouth of the dark.

Rotary-Dialing Numbers

Entombed in a room painted powder blue
cloud soft slippers cozied her feet
cotton house dress swaddled her form
propped up on a firm TV cushion
with a tall iced-vodka drink
washing down a fistful of pills
while rotary-dialing numbers
trying to connect to times gone by
re-call life as perfect as it was
a simple, happy-ever-after passion play—
beautiful girl winds up with handsome man
and an ailing cat she'd nursed back to health
a loving family chattering cheerily
in a clattered chaos of chairs and cooking
Thanksgiving dishes;
baby cooing on her lap
banging a spoon, others clunked by plates
records turning finger-snapping music round
glad noises now but a remnant soundtrack
to that posthumously precious pictured past.
embalmed in a room painted powder blue
the phone line was cast over and over into
that murky sea of yesteryear in an attempt
to recatch that which—in thoughtless youth—
had been (not discarded) but let slip away,
a glorious reality irretrievable
except on the distant shores of sleep
where only a few were freely ferried.
She sipped a toast and continued taking pills:
the hundred 56th was for a father who snuck out on foot
the hundred 57th for a mother who died by her own hand
the hundred 58th for the handsome man let slip away;
and one pill each for: the glory of his charisma,
the magic of his smile,

the titillation of his flattery,
the warmth of his arms,
and one for every good time they'd missed,
there was one for each child she had lost
and ached to hold but couldn't
through the barricade of consciousness

Pill ~ Swig ~ Pill ~ Swig ~ Phone

imprisoned by phobias in a room painted powder blue
in the middle of once sought after suburbia
ever more slowly, she was rotary-dialing numbers
dialing and dialing: calling for help, calling out loud
for someone to talk to, for the sound of a voice,
now no one in particular, anyone would do, but
all she got was ringing and ringing and ringing
on the phone in her hand and the halls of her mind
as she refilled her tall iced-vodka drink
cloud soft slippers cozied her feet
her form swaddled in a cotton house dress

propped up with a TV cushion to keep her
hair freshly coiffed for friends in her thoughts.
She took one more pill, the hundred 78th or 87th
and wait. Wait! Wait! The ringing stopped.
company appeared angelic faces full of smiles
with arms outstretched; she let go of the receiver,
let it dangle, let the cord spin, a voice was
repeating: Hello? Hello? Hello? Hello?

Missing

On the road; no permanent address.

Missing person?
Oh, it's Me.
Last seen at two in the a.m.
Half awake,
Fully nude
clothed in chaos
Traveling somewhere
East of Eden
West of Jesus,
South of San-i-ty
Avoiding the damn Last Exit.

I wanna go home,
wherever it is,
though no one waits,
not siblings or friends,
neighbors or family
but that home
houses my clothes and
books and memories
all my things acquired
so far. There's that cozy
comfort of familiarity
in all the stuff that's me.

Away from there
Negativity lurks in
windows that reflect me
as worthless,
fill my head with the
thought
.

I'm better off dead.
My road back is
Deserted
few to notice
Missing person: me.

Those that do
ask with their eyes,
What's wrong with her?
Is she a danger?
Is she sick?
Is she a druggie?
Is she blue?
Is she lost?
Or has she lost it?
And they walk by.

I wanna go home,
wherever it is,
though no one waits,
not siblings or friends,
neighbors or family
but that home
houses my clothes and
books and memories
all my things acquired
so far. There's that cozy
comfort of familiarity
in all the stuff that's me.

~ ~ ~

Reference

~ ~ ~

❀ Books consulted:

Alvarez, A. *The Savage god: A study of suicide*, New York: Random House. (1979).

Beck, A. T., Rush, A., Shaw, B., & Emery, G. *Cognitive therapy of depression.* New York: Guilford Press, 1979.

Brown, G., Have, T., Henriques, G., Xie, S., Hollander, J., & Durkheim, *Émile, Suicide: A study in sociology.* (J. A. Spaulding & G. Simpson, Trans.) New York: The Free Press 1951. (Original work published 1897)

Freud, Sigmund, (1957). Mourning and Melancholia. In J. Strachey (Ed.), The standard edition of the complete works of Sigmund Freud (Vol. 14, p. 237-260). London: Hogarth Press. (Original work published in 1917)

Lester, D. *Psychache, depression, and personality,* 2000.

Amanda Smith, ed., *Hostage to Fortune: The Letters of Joseph P. Kennedy* (New York, Viking, 2001)

Baker, C. (1969). *Ernest Hemingway: A life story.* New York: Charles Scribner's Sons.

Brockett, L.P., *The Life and Times of Abraham Lincoln*

Burgess, A. (1978). *Ernest Hemingway.* New York: Thames &c Hudson.

Gibson, Barbara & Schwarz, *Ted, Rose Kennedy And Her Family-The Best And Worst Of Their Lives And Times,* Birch Lane Press, 1995

Glendinning, Victoria (2006). *Leonard Woolf: a Biography.* New York: Free Press.

Hemingway, E. M. (1929). *A Farewell to Arms.* New York: Charles Scribner's Sons.

Hemingway, E. M. (1935). *Green Hills of Africa.* New York: Charles Scribner's Sons.

Hemingway, E. M. (1952). *The Old Man and the Sea.* New York: Charles Scribner's Sons.

Hemingway, E. M. (1964). *A Moveable Feast.* New York: Charles Scribner's Sons.

Hemingway, E. M. (1981). *Ernest Hemingway: Selected Letters: 1917-1961.* (C. Baker, Ed.). New York: Charles Scribner's Sons.

Hotchner, A. E. (1966). *Papa Hemingway.* New York: Random House.

Hotchner, A. E., *Papa Hemingway: A Personal Memoir,* Random House, 1966

J.G. Holland, *The Life of Abraham Lincoln* (Springfield, Mass: Gurdon Bill, 1865).

Jamison, K. R. (1993). *Touched with fire: Manic-depressive illness and the artistic temperament.* New York: Simon & Schuster.

Kessler, Ronald *The Sins of the Father: Joseph P. Kennedy and the Dynasty He Founded,* Grand Central Publishing. 1996

Kirsch, Irving, *The Emperor's New Drugs: Exploding the Antidepressant Myth.* Random House, 2009.

Leenaars, A. (2004). *Psychotherapy with Suicidal People.* New York: John Wiley & Sons.

Lester, D. (Ed.) (2004). *Katie's diary.* New York: Brunner-Routledge.

Lynn, K. S. (1987). *Hemingway.* New York: Simon & Schuster.

Malinowsky, Bronislaw, Baloma; *the Spirits of the Dead in the Trobriand,* 1922.

Mellow, J. R. (1992). *Hemingway: A life without consequences.* Boston: Houghton Mifflin.

Monroe Marilyn, *My Story,* 1954

Pearce, Brian Louis, *Virginia Woolf and the Bloomsbury Group in Twickenham,* Borough of Twickenham History Society, 2007.

Price, W. *Nutrition and Physical Degeneration,* Keats Publishing, 1943.

Shneidman, Dr. Edwin S., *The Suicidal Mind,* 1998

Shneidman, E. & Farberow, N. (Eds.) (1957). *Clues to Suicide.* New York: McGraw-Hill.

W.H. Auden *The Age of Anxiety.* 1948, William H. Herdon, Lincoln and Ann Rutledge and the Pioneers of New Salem (Herrin, Ill.: Trovillion Private Press, 1945).

Williams, Tennessee, *Memoirs* 1975 Allen, J. (1999).

Yalom, I. D., & Yalom, M. (1971). Ernest Hemingway: A psychiatric view. *Archives of General Psychiatry, 24,* 485-494.

Vincent van Gogh to his brother:

Mon cher frère,

Merci de ta lettre d'aujourd'hui et du billet de 50 fr. qu'elle contenait.

Je voudrais peutêtre t'écrire sur bien des chôses mais d'abord l'envie m'en a tellement passée, puis j'en sens l'inutilité.

J'espère que tu auras retrouvé ces messieurs dans de bonnes dispositions à ton égard.

Pour ce qui est de l'état de paix dans ton ménage, je suis autant convaincu de la possibilité de la conserver que des orages qui la menacent.

Je préfère ne pas oublier le peu de francais que je sais et certes ne saurais voir l'utilité d'approfondir le tort ou la raison dans des discussions éventuelles de part ou autre. Seulement cela m'intéresserait pas.

Ici les chôses vont vite – Dries, toi et moi n'en sommes nous pas un peu plus convaincus, le sentons nous pas un peu davantage que ces dames. Tant mieux pour elles – mais enfin causer à tête reposée, nous n'y comptons même pas.–

En ce qui me regarde je m'applique sur mes toiles avec toute mon attention, je cherche à faire aussi bien que de certains peintres que j'ai beaucoup aimé et admiré.–

Ce qu'il me semble en revenant – c'est que les peintres eux mêmes sont de plus en plus aux abois.–

Bon mais le moment de chercher à leur faire comprendre l'utilité d'une union n'est il pas un peu passé déjà. D'autre part une union, se formerait elle, sombrerait si le reste doive sombrer. Alors tu me dirais peutêtre que des marchands s'uniraient pour les impressionistes; ce serait bien passager. Enfin il me semble que l'initiative personnelle demeure inefficace, et experience faite, la recommencerait-on?

J'ai constaté avec plaisir que le Gauguin de Bretagne que j'ai vu etait très beau et il me semble que les autres qu'il a fait là-bas doivent l'être aussi.–

Vincent van Gogh to his brother:

My dear brother,

Thanks for your letter of today and for the 50-franc note it contained.

I'd perhaps like to write to you about many things, but first the desire has passed to such a degree, then I sense the pointlessness of it.

I hope that you'll have found those gentlemen favourably disposed towards you.

As regards the state of peace in your household, I'm just as convinced of the possibility of preserving it as of the storms that threaten it.

I prefer not to forget the little French I know, and certainly wouldn't see the point of delving deeper into the rights or wrongs in any discussions on one side or the other. It's just that this wouldn't interest me.

Things go quickly here – aren't Dries, you and I a little more convinced of that, don't we feel it a little more than those ladies. So much the better for them – but anyway, talking with rested minds, we can't even count on that.

As for myself, I'm applying myself to my canvases with all my attention, I'm trying to do as well as certain painters whom I've liked and admired a great deal.

What seems to me on my return – is that the painters themselves are increasingly at bay.

Very well. But has the moment to make them understand the utility of a union not rather passed already? On the other hand a union, if it were formed, would go under if the rest went under.

Then you'd perhaps tell me that dealers would unite for the Impressionists; that would be very fleeting. Anyway it seems to me that personal initiative remains ineffective, and having done the experiment, would one begin it again?

Peut-être verras tu ce croquis du jardin de Daubigny – c'est une de mes toiles les plus voulues– j'y joins un croquis de vieux chaumes et les croquis de 2 toiles de 30 représentant d'immenses étendues de blé après la pluie. Hirschig a demandé de te prier de vouloir bien lui commander la liste de couleurs ci jointe chez le même marchand des couleurs que tu m'envoies. Tasset peut les lui envoyer directement à lui contre remboursement mais alors il faudrait lui accorder les 20%.
Ce qui sera le plus simple.
Ou bien tu les joindrais à l'envoi de couleurs pour moi en ajoutant la facture ou en me disant combien en est le montant et alors il t'enverrait l'argent à toi. Ici on ne peut pas en trouver de bonnes de couleurs.
J'ai simplifié ma commande à moi jusqu'à un minimum bien raide.
Hirsching commence à comprendre un peu il m'a semblé, il a fait le portrait du vieux maitre d'école qu'il lui a donné, bien – et puis il a des etudes de paysage qui sont comme les Konink qui sont chez toi à peu près comme couleur. Cela deviendra peutêtre tout à fait comme cela ou comme les choses de Voerman que nous avons vues ensemble.
à bientot. Porte toi bien et bonne chance dans les affaires &c.
bien le bonjour à Jo et poignées de main en pensée.

        b. à v.

Perhaps you'll see this croquis of Daubigny's garden – it's one of my most deliberate canvases – to it I'm adding a croquis of old thatched roofs and the croquis of 2 no. 30 canvases depicting immense stretches of wheat after the rain. Hirschig asked me to ask you please to order the attached list of colours for him from the same paint store you sent me. Tasset can send them directly to him, cash on delivery, but then he would have to be given the 20%.

Which would be simplest.

Or you'd put them into the order for me, adding the invoice or telling me how much they cost, and then he'd send you the money. Here one can't find anything good in the way of colours. I've simplified my own order to a very bare minimum.

Hirschig is beginning to understand a little, it has seemed to me, he's done the portrait of the old schoolmaster, which he gave him, good – and then he has landscape studies which are a little like the Konings at your place as regards colour. It will become completely like that, perhaps, or like the things by Voerman that we saw together.

More soon. Look after yourself, and good luck in business etc. Warm regards to Jo, and handshakes in thought.

Yours truly,
Vincent.

Marilyn Monroe's death/FBI File

A note of romanticism plays along with the tune the world sings that Marilyn Monroe killed herself. The idea that the beautiful, talented iconic actor could have been murdered is too unpalatable for her admirers. Yet, conspiracy theories abound. At the top of the list are: She was killed because she knew too much about UFO's; the Mafia put a hit on her to get back at the Kennedy's, Robert Kennedy, along with FBI director J. Edgar Hoover and Peter Lawford staged her death; her doctor gave her a hot shot to the heart and as Joe DiMaggio told author, Rock Positano, "I always knew who killed her, but I didn't want to start a revolution in this country. She told me someone would do her in, but I kept quiet..."[212] and "they did in my poor Marilyn. She didn't know what hit her." Her friend, actor, Debbie Reynolds said she and Marilyn attended the same church, that she was quite religious. She felt Marilyn's relationships with John and Robert Kennedy put her at risk. "I saw her two days before she died and warned her to be careful...I believe she was murdered because too many people were afraid the truth would come out." While she purportedly suffered from suicidal ideation that does not mean suicide is imminent, just that the annoying idea plagues one. The mountain of evidence surrounding her death indicates she did not kill herself.

An LA prosecutor, John W. Miner, who investigated her death, heard sessions psychologist, Dr. Ralph Greenson had played tapes between him and Marilyn. In an interview with ABC News, he states, they were those prior to her "suicide," and that "No reasonable person could possibly think that the person who made those tapes killed herself." He reports her to be planning to break up with Robert Kennedy and focus more on acting, Shakespeare. In fact, Marilyn had long longed to get out from under the studios and break away from the mindless sex-kitten roles they chose for her. In December 1954, she formed Marilyn Monroe Productions, Inc. with photographer Milton Greene.

---

[212] Positano, Rock, Dr.,"Dinner with DiMaggio," Simon & Schuster, 2017.

Who would want kill her? Her well-known, well-sought after, "little red diary" which she often read to Dr. Greenson, by his account, held secrets whispered by the political leaders such as the Kennedys. She had drawn the attention of both the CIA and the FBI. Rather strangely, one of heir files lists her death on March 4 and reads that Marilyn Monroe's personal secretary and press agent Pat Newcombe "were coordinating a plan to "induce suicide." [Whatever that means.] Supposedly, she died from an overdose of sleeping pills, yet an autopsy proved her stomach contained none. I, personally, do not believe she took her own life.

May she Rest in Peace.

FBI notes on Marilyn's production company.

MARILYN MONROE The Bureau furnished the NYO an article concerning MARILYN MONROE appearing in "The Washington Post" of 4/15/56 in its magazine section, "Parade."

This article, written by LLOYD SHEARER, "Parade" West Coast Correspondent, indicated that the MARILYN MONROE Productions was formed, with MARILYN MONROE, President and MILTON GREENE, Vice-President and Treasurer.

The article further indicated that GREENE was, a photographer for "Look" magazine, 34 years old, is married to AMY GREENE and spends considerable time in Hollywood and NY. According to the article MARILYN MONROE came to NY in 1955 and moved in with the GREENES. She appeared on the EDWARD R. MURROW program "Person to Person" from the home of the GREENES, in Westport, Connecticut.

who has furnished reliable information in the past, furnished the following information on 4/26/56:

Records of December 20, 1954 show Marilyn Monroe Productions, Inc., chartered New York laws, with 200 shares no par value common stock. The object, entertainment, publishing, and theatrical productions and photography.

"Life" Magazine Photographs?

3 - Bureau (100-422103) (UNSUB:
    (1) - MARILYN MONROE)
2 - New Haven (RM)
2 - Los Angeles (RM)
1 - New York (100-127997)
JHS:PDD
(8)

NOT RECORDED
162 MAY 1 1956

1/05-40018-

CONFIDENTIAL

63 MAY 4 - 1956

Reference

The following: Transcription of typed FBI agent's report, barely legible in places and blocked out in others, of Marilyn's association with Robert Kennedy and her suicide.

"Robert Kennedy had been having an romantic [blacked out] sex affair over a period of time with Marilyn Monroe [deceased]. He had met her, the first time [ill.] being arranged by his sister and brother-in-law, Mr. and Mrs. Peter Lawford. Robert Kennedy had been spending much time in Hollywood during the last part of 1961 and early [ill] in collaboration with his trying to have a film made of his back dealing with the crime investigations. [three lines blacked out.]

Robert Kennedy was deeply involved emotionally with Marilyn Monroe, and had repeatedly promised to divorce his wife to Marry Marilyn. Eventually Marilyn realized that Bobby had no intention of marrying her, and about this time, 20th Century Fox studios had decided to cancel her contract. She had become very unreliable, [illegible] set, [ill.]. In addition, the studio was in financial difficulty due to the large expenditures [ill] in the filming of "Cleopatra".

The studio notified Marilyn that they were cancelling her contract. This was right in the middle of a picture she was making. They decided to replace her with actress Lee Remick. Marilyn telephoned Robert Kennedy from her home in Brentwood California, person-to-person, at the Department of Justice, in Washington D.C. to tell him the bad news. Robert Kennedy told her not to worry about the contract – he would take care of everything. When nothing was done, she again called him from her home to the Department of Justice, person-to-person, and on this occasion, they had unpleasant words. She was reported to have threatened to make public their affair. On the day that Marilyn died, Robert Kennedy was in town and registered at the Beverly Hills Hotel. [three lines blacked out]

Peter Lawford [two lines blacked out]...knew from Marilyn's friends that she often made suicide threats and that she was inclined to fake a suicide attempt in order to arouse sympathy. Lawford is reported as having made "special arrangements" with Marilyn's psychiatrist, Dr. Ralph Greenson of Beverly Hills. The psychiatrist was treating Marilyn for her emotional problems and getting her off the use of barbiturates. On her last visit to him, he prescribed Seconal tablets, and gave her a prescription for so... of them which was unusual in quantity especially since she saw him frequently.

On the date of her death, March 4, 1962, her housekeeper put the bottle of pills on the night table. It is reported that Marilyn's personal secretary and press agent, Pat Necombe were cooperating in the plan to induce suicide.
END

The world will probably never know the truth.

CIA file notes regarding the ongoing conspiracy surrounding Marilyn Monroe's death.

Twenty years after she died, Marilyn Monroe is still allowed no peace.

Rewards of up to $100,000 have been offered for her so-called red diary, a private detective believes she was killed by a dissident faction of the CIA

and a former coroner's aide claims he was coerced into signing her death certificate.

Robert Slatzer, author of "The Life and Curious Death of Marilyn Monroe," published in 1974, told reporters that in the last summer of her life Miss Monroe was having an affair with Senator Kennedy.

He said Miss Monroe showed him her diary, which included details of her relationship with Kennedy, who was then U.S. attorney general, and information about the CIA.

Slatzer said Kennedy broke off his relationship with Miss Monroe two weeks before her death. "This was a woman who couldn't take rejection," Slatzer said.

He said on the night before she died she told him by telephone if she did not hear from Kennedy soon she would call a press conference "and blow the lid."

Michael Speriglio, a member of a leading Los Angeles private detective agency who said he had been investigating Miss Monroe's for 10 years, offered a $10,000 reward for the diary.

He said he had evidence, which he did not specify, that the diary included entries of Kennedy telling Miss Monroe of a CIA plot to kill Cuban leader Fidel Castro.

He told a press conference he had uncovered through sources a plot organized by the CIA to kidnap Miss Monroe and take her to a "safe house" in Virginia, where the CIA has its headquarters.

"The faction intended to make known later Miss Monroe had suffered a nervous breakdown so no one would accept what she said," Speriglio said.

But, he said, he believed what he called a dissident CIA faction got to Miss Monroe first and murdered her.

FBI file notes requesting Ernest Hemingway's book to be stopped.

Letter confirming the FBI's communication with Hemingway's doctors confirming the author's suspicion of their tracking him.

FD-36 (Rev. 12-13-56)

Mr. Tolson
Mr. Mohr
Mr. Parsons
Mr. Belmont
Mr. Callahan
Mr. DeLoach
Mr. Malone
Mr. McGuire
Mr. Rosen
Mr. Tamm
Mr. Trotter
Mr. W.C.Sullivan
Tele. Room
Mr. Ingram
Miss Gandy

F B I

Date: **1/13/61**

Transmit the following in _____ **PLAIN** _____
(Type in plain text or code)

Via _____ **AIRTEL** _____
(Priority or Method of Mailing)

TO: DIRECTOR, FBI   PERSONAL ATTENTION

FROM: SAC, MINNEAPOLIS

RE: ERNEST HEMINGWAY
INFORMATION CONCERNING

ERNEST HEMINGWAY, the author, has been a patient at Mayo
Clinic, Rochester, Minnesota, and is presently at St. Mary's
Hospital in that city. He has been at the Clinic for several
weeks, and is described as a problem. He is seriously ill,
both physically and mentally, and at one time the doctors
were considering giving him electro-shock therapy treatments.

[   ] Mayo Clinic, advised to
eliminate publicity and contacts by newsmen, the Clinic had
suggested that Mr. HEMINGWAY register under the alias GEORGE
SEVIER. [   ] stated that Mr. HEMINGWAY is now
worried about his registering under an assumed name, and is
concerned about an FBI investigation. [   ] stated that
inasmuch as this worry was interfering with the treatments
of Mr. HEMINGWAY, he desired authorization to tell HEMINGWAY
that the FBI was not concerned with his registering under
an assumed name. [   ] was advised that there was no
objection.

3 - Bureau
1 - Minneapolis
WHW:RSK
(4)
cc - DeLoach

64-23312-18

11 JAN 24 1961

52 JAN 31 1961

Approved: _____   Sent _____ M   Per _____
Special Agent in Charge

INTAKE QUESTIONNAIRES

These include the usual questions: name, medical history, true-false or tick-the-box stuff. The intensely personal questions reflect insensitivity and ignorance on the part of the medical community. When I was a defendant in a law suit, I was astonished to learn that psychiatric records, despite confidentiality laws, could be requested. Thus one could easily lose one's job, insurance or friends should even the suggestion of a mental illness get out; thus, one should beware and discuss privacy concerns with one's doctor.

EXCEPTIONS TO CONFIDENTIALITY RULES

• Sometimes, the law authorizes us to disclose information about you without your permission.
• To qualified personnel for audit, program evaluation, or research; for example, patient surveys.
• In response to court orders that comply with the standards for the type of record covered by the order.
This is not an actual form but questions I remember from several; hence, the random numbering.

SAMPLE QUESTIONS.
Race.[213]

    [ ] African-Amer.
    [ ] American Indian or Alaskan Native
    [ ] Arab American / Arab / Persian
    [ ] Asian American / Asian
    [ ] East Indian
    [ ] European American / White / Caucasian
    [ ] Hispanic / Latino / Latina
    [ ] Native Hawaiian or Pacific Islander
    [ ] Multi-racial

---

[213] As a student of anthropology I learned race is a socio-cultural construct, a myth of biology that, according to DNA, does not exist. Most recently this has been proven again by the world-renowned geneticist, anthropologist, author and explorer-in-Residence at the National Geographic Society, Dr. Spencer Wells.

Questions that begin with "ON A SCALE OF" are popular, per-haps due to doctor's scientific training.

> On a scale of 1-5 (1 = low, 5 = high).
> Rate your overall level of happiness _____
> Rate quality of present relationship/marriage_____
> Rate your alcohol consumption_____
> Rate you overall level of self-esteem_____
> Rate your ability to sleep_____

The restriction of 1-5 led me to wonder how they could assess those who were bipolar. Wouldn't they need -10 and + 20? Other numbers stood out.

15.   Have you every filed or been involved in any litigation? Please explain.
Legally a full explanation is usually not possible. What do they need this information for?
33.   Do you currently want to kill someone?
I laughed and contemplated whether the time I found my boy-friend in bed with my neighbor counted. (Does anyone actually answer that?)
63. Have you ever had feelings or thoughts that you didn't want to live? ( ) Yes ( ) No. If YES, please answer the following.

1.   Do you currently feel that you don't want to live? ( ) Yes ( ) No
2.   How often do you have these thoughts?
3.   When was the last time you had thoughts of dying?
4.   Has anything happened recently to make you feel this way?
5.   On a scale of 1 to 10, (ten being strongest) how strong is your desire to kill yourself currently?
6.   Would anything make it better?
7.   Have you ever thought about *how* you to kill yourself?
8.   Is the method you would use readily available?
9.   Have you planned a time for this?
10. Is there anything that would stop you?

11. Do you feel hopeless and /or worthless?
12. Have you ever tried to kill or harm yourself before?

64. In your life, have you experienced anything, frightening, horrible, or upsetting that gave you nightmares or it made you feel numb or detached from others, activities, or my surroundings. If yes, describe in the space provided.

Good Company

As a depressive, you are in the company of brilliant, accomplished individuals. Many of them speak publicly about depression and how they cope with it.

Alan Alda, six-time Emmy and Golden Globe award-winner
Billy Joel, a six-time Grammy Award-winning musician.
Brooke Shields, actor
Carrie Fisher, the actor who played Princess Leia in *Star Wars*.
Diana, Princess of Wales
Dorothy Hamill, Gold medal figure skating, 1976 Olympics
Ellen DeGeneres, Comedian, TV host, television producer
Sir Elton John, British, composer, pianist, record producer
Ernest Hemingway, author, Pulitzer Prize and Nobel Prize
Eugene O'Neill, Nobel Prize, *Long Days Journey into Night*
Greg Louganis, gold medals in diving 1984 and 1988 Olympics
Halle Berry, Academy Award for *Monster's Ball*
Jane Pauley, NBC news broadcaster since the age of 25, has been candid about her depression and bipolar illnesses.
Jim Carrey, comedian, actor.
John Nash, a Nobel Prize winner in Economics in 1994
Judy Collins, singer and songwriter.
Kay Redfield Jamison, psychiatrist and professor of psychiatry
Leo Tolstoy, Russian author.
Ludwig van Beethoven, German composer and pianist.
Mike Wallace, Journalist and news anchor.
Patty Duke, an actor, winner of the Academy Award for *The Miracle Worker*,
Tennessee Williams was a Pulitzer Prize-winning playwright,
Vivien Leigh, actor.
Winston Churchill, former Prime Minister of Great Britain, Nobel Prize-winning writer.
Woody Allen, director, screenwriter, comedian, musician

❀DEPRESSION IS A JOURNEY

These are reminders that can be cut out and put on the fridge or your computer or by your bed or…

REMIND YOURSELF

✂ ···

I HAVE PERMISSION TO BE DEPRESSED and that means

I MUST BE PROACTIVE.

✂ ···

I WILL GET UP EVERYDAY, WASH AND DRESS.
(Even if I don't feel like it. I can do it.)

TALK ABOUT DEPRESSION,

WITH THE RIGHT PERSON/PEOPLE.
(I can let my friends and family know, "I am looking for help."
They care about me and are important.)

I CAN TRY MEDICATION
(I must be patient. It takes time to work, usually a month.)

✂ ··

I WILL STAY CONNECTED TO OTHERS.
(I will accept invites, even if it is to come and sit.)

I WILL WALK AT LEAST ONCE A DAY.

I KNOW DEPRESSION SLOWS DOWN TIME,
(It only feels like I have been down forever.)

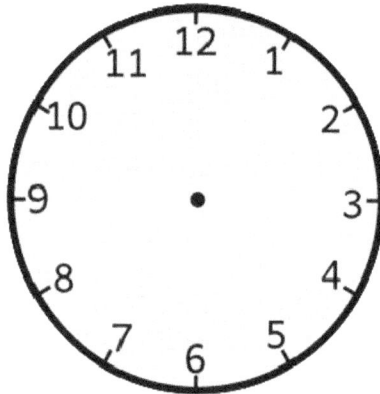

I WILL READ

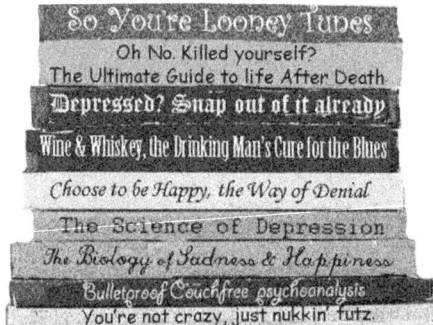

So You're Looney Tunes
Oh No. Killed yourself?
The Ultimate Guide to life After Death
Depressed? Snap out of it already
Wine & Whiskey, the Drinking Man's Cure for the Blues
Choose to be Happy, the Way of Denial
The Science of Depression
The Biology of Sadness & Happiness
Bulletproof Couchfree psychoanalysis
You're not crazy, just nukkin' futz.

I WILL TRY WRITING A JOURNAL

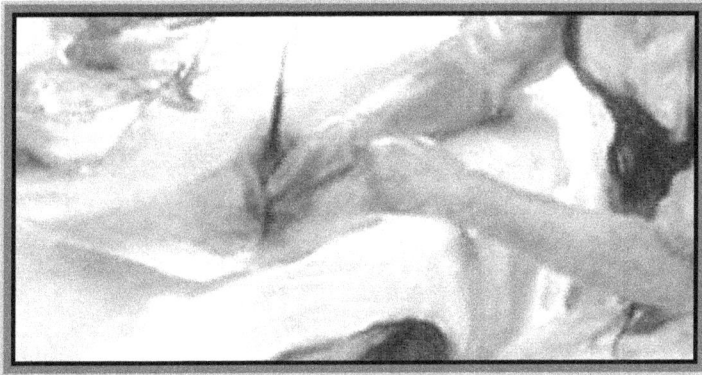

✂ ··

Breathe

✂ ··

I WILL TRY TO TURN THE LIGHT ON MYSELF, NOT WAIT FOR IT TO APPEAR.

✂ ··

Eat

to feed my body, not depression.

Laugh

deliberately for no reason.

I DO NOT HAVE TO PUT ON A HAPPY FACE, BUT I SHOULD BE CIVIL.

I HAVE PERMISSION TO FEEL SAD.

EASIER TO COPE W/ BEING SAD THAN TRYING TO COPE WITH BEING DEAD.

✂ ··· ...

If I must, I WILL LIVE LIKE LINCOLN
become comfortable with depression.

Photo: Eve Arnold, April 1955, at Abraham Lincoln Museum.

🌸 FRIENDS AND FAMILY OF DEPRESSIVES[214]

I WILL VISIT OR CALL MY DEPRESSED FRIEND.

I WILL INVITE MY DEPRESSED FRIEND TO TEA/COFFEE
OR FOR A WALK.

I WILL ACCEPT MY DEPRESSED FRIEND'S SADNESS,
BUT
I WILL ENCOURAGE MY FRIEND TO SEEK HELP.
(I will suggest s/he get help on occasion but not in a hostile, fed
up way.)

I WILL MAKE A LIST OF THINGS WE CAN DISCUSS.

I WILL ASK MYSELF, "WHAT DO I KNOW ABOUT
DEPRESSION?" I WILL REMIND MYSELF, I AM NOT
QUALIFIED TO TREAT DEPRESSION.

THEIR depression should not take over our friendship

THEIR THERAPY IS NOT MY BUSINESS.

I WILL SET BOUNDARIES.
This means if the friend is mistreating you, you must tell him. "I
want to be here for you, but if you can't control yourself a little, I
will have to go." If the friend is calling you at all hours, you can
answer. Say, "This is not a good time. We are not thinking
clearly. Let's get together tomorrow after we have had some
sleep. OK? What time is good for you?"

I UNDERSTAND MY FRIEND MUST
BE PROACTIVE IN GETTING HELP.

---

[214] Unless the Depressive is a minor, these are good guidelines. For minors,
parents or guardians must exercise the right to insist, at least on professional
psychiatric assessment, probably more than one. Urge the minor to be open
and honest.

ALL SUICIDE THREATS ARE REAL.

Every ten minutes a person commits suicide. It is the 10th cause of death in the overall population and the 3rd among young people 15-24.

If you suspect a person is in immediate danger of self-harm, call 911. If you have not heard from them for a while, you can request the police to conduct a wellness check.

SUICIDE CRISIS HOTLINE
1-800-784-2433 or 1-800-273-8255
In the United States:

*Notice:

While researched and quoted, the perspectives on mental health stated by the author, Winchinchala, are for informational purposes only and not intended as specific psychiatric/medical advice or a substitute for professional psychiatric medical treatment or diagnoses.

.

www.ingramcontent.com/pod-product-compliance
Lightning Source LLC
Chambersburg PA
CBHW031147270326
41931CB00006B/171